"*The Jonathan Effect* is not only a blueprint for social action, it is a reflection of an author who does more than write: he lives his philosophies and employs his own call to action. With this book, Mike Tenbusch dismantles a current crisis with an age-old approach—begin with caring, trust your beliefs, get out to where the problem is, and never give up on children. I've seen it work, as I've seen Mike work. The world is a better place as a result."
Mitch Albom, author of *Tuesdays with Morrie*

"I'm very particular about how people write about Detroit, my hometown. As a fellow native Detroiter, Mike's book was a breath of fresh air. I was moved to tears as he described the violence in his community, as it rang all too familiar. But his message of hope about the role that churches have in helping to transform schools and communities will inspire all who read it. Beyond inspiration, *The Jonathan Effect* will help communities identify practical steps to becoming a part of the immediate and long-term solutions. This is a must-read for anyone who cares deeply about urban communities, poverty, schools, and our nation's children."
Nicole Baker Fulgham, founder and president, The Expectations Project, author of *Educating All God's Children*

"This is a moving, inspiring, and important book. Mike Tenbusch has a powerful message for anyone who despairs about the students struggling in our nation's worst schools: these students aren't doomed. But the best solution starts outside the school. With you, in fact. Read on and answer the call!"
Dan Heath, coauthor of *New York Times* bestsellers *Switch, Made to Stick,* and *Decisive*

"Mike Tenbusch lays out a beautiful and simple expression of the gospel at work in Detroit—churches mobilizing people to love and serve children by investing in schools. This church-school partnership piece is key to loving and serving our cities in Jesus' name, and this book and these stories will inspire more churches to get involved, believing God will change lives as a result."
Kevin Palau, president, Luis Palau Association, and author of *Unlikely: Setting Aside our Differences to Live Out the Gospel*

"The world has watched Detroit's rebirth into a thriving, vibrant city. Yet we risk losing it all if we leave our city's schools and children behind. Mike Tenbusch offers real solutions. As vice president of United Way, he has worked with teachers, administrators, and students to help reimagine and rebuild the city's education system. He showed me how businesses can help through a sustained commitment to partnership, personal connection, and putting students first. As a result, GM's partnership with Detroit-area schools to increase graduation rates achieved incredible results and rewards beyond measure. Mike's compelling, engaging book offers inspiration and instruction for companies and organizations to do the same, and I encourage them to do so."

Mark Reuss, executive vice president, Global Product Development, General Motors Company

"Mike Tenbusch expertly translates his enthusiasm and passion for youth into a practical book with direct application for educators, child advocates, policy makers, and the evangelical church. While set in Detroit, this story is universal. Tenbusch offers a line of sight to a faction of youth who feel forgotten and invisible in a world where your zip code defines your destiny. This book recounts how collective leadership can be transformational in unleashing the collective genius of urban youth. It shares how the caring capital of a community can be deployed and leveraged at the individual level, institutional level and systems level to untangle the snare of underperforming schools, concentrated poverty, and unsafe neighborhoods."

Tonya Allen, President and CEO, The Skillman Foundation

THE JONATHAN EFFECT

*Helping Kids and Schools Win
the Battle Against Poverty*

MIKE TENBUSCH

IVP Books

An imprint of InterVarsity Press
Downers Grove, Illinois

InterVarsity Press
P.O. Box 1400, Downers Grove, IL 60515-1426
ivpress.com
email@ivpress.com

InterVarsity Press® is the book-publishing division of InterVarsity Christian Fellowship/USA®, a movement of students and faculty active on campus at hundreds of universities, colleges and schools of nursing in the United States of America, and a member movement of the International Fellowship of Evangelical Students. For information about local and regional activities, visit intervarsity.org.

All Scripture quotations, unless otherwise indicated, are taken from THE HOLY BIBLE, NEW INTERNATIONAL VERSION®, NIV® Copyright © 1973, 1978, 1984, 2011 by Biblica, Inc.™ Used by permission. All rights reserved worldwide.

While the stories in this book are true, some names and identifying information may have been changed to protect the privacy of individuals.

Figure 6.1: Photo by Walter V. Marshall. Used by permission

Cover design: Cindy Kiple
Interior design: Beth McGill
Images: © Sean_Warren/iStockphoto

ISBN 978-0-8308-4477-7 (print)
ISBN 978-0-8308-8101-7 (digital)

Printed in the United States of America ∞

Library of Congress Cataloging-in-Publication Data

A catalog record for this book is available from the Library of Congress.

P	20	19	18	17	16	15	14	13	12	11	10	9	8	7	6	5	4	3	2	1
Y	33	32	31	30	29	28	27	26	25	24	23	22	21	20	19	18	17	16			

To

Fr. Frank Canfield, SJ,

the best example of Christ to me and thousands

of boys trained to become men for others by the

Jesuits in Detroit, Toledo and Cleveland

over the last fifty years.

And to

Johnathon Matthews,

the living Jonathan to the young people of

the Academy of Public Leadership at Cody,

and the inspiration for this book.

Contents

Preface

The phone in my mother's room blared at 6:15 on a Sunday morning. It was for me. I was a college senior at home for Thanksgiving break. I had been out drinking the night before with a college friend, Karla, who lived down the street. I stumbled into my mom's room trying to wake up as I walked.

Karla was on the line. "Mike, can you come over? They broke into our house last night."

"Aw, man, I'm so sorry. Are you okay?" I said.

"It's my dad, Mike," she replied. "They shot him."

"Oh my God, Karla," I said, "I'll be right there. Is he okay?"

"He's dead." She sobbed. "They killed him." She cried into the phone and then hung up.

I threw on a sweatshirt and some jeans, and made the longest two-block walk of my life.

Police clustered around the door and front room of Karla's home as I made my way through. Court testimony later revealed that the killers were hiding in the bushes across the street. These same two men had broken into a home the week before, bound and gagged a man, and assaulted his wife in front of him.

But all I knew at that time was that Karla and her college roommate, who had come home with her for the weekend, were sitting numb at the kitchen table, and I had been called to comfort them.

This was not the first time that murder had rocked our block. When I was in kindergarten, my classmate who lived a few doors down from Karla came home to find his mother lying dead on the kitchen floor. She had been beaten by the man who gave her a ride home from a car dealership.

When I was a sophomore in high school, a sixteen-year-old girl who lived three houses down was shot dead by the fifteen-year-old father of their newborn child. Her sister was also shot but survived; that night, at age thirteen, she became the mother of her nephew.

The murder that hurt the most happened that same fall. About a mile from my home, at about midnight Melody Rucker was standing on her porch waving goodbye to the last of her friends who had come to celebrate her sweet-sixteen birthday party at her home. A passing car, filled with fifteen-year-old boys who had been denied entrance to the party a few hours earlier, fired a shotgun at her house. The blast struck Melody, who died in her father's arms.

Melody was the popular girl at Benedictine High School, a Catholic school across the street from my grade school. Most of the kids I knew loved Melody and wanted revenge, including me. Her murder was one of those tragedies that saddened a city. A few days later, her killers were caught, one of whom turned out to be a friend of mine. How do you exact revenge on a person you love?

In 1987, the year I graduated from high school, the impact of crack and of gangs that used kids to sell drugs had ravished the city. That year, 365 children aged sixteen and under were shot, and forty-three of them died. I remember those numbers because it meant that one child was shot every day of the year, and forty-three was also the number of people killed in the Detroit riots of 1967, two years before I was born. As a kid growing up, it felt like the adults around me were still trying to finish the arguments that fueled the riots rather than focusing on solutions to the everyday violence.

So by the time I sat with Karla and her roommate to comfort them on that Sunday morning in 1990, random killings had become a part of life for me. They hardened me and confounded me at the same time. I went to God often in these times, asking him why he allows these things to happen. And what I heard back was, "This isn't my will" and "You can do something about this."

I've been consumed by that challenge for the last twenty-five years. In my first job out of college, I taught welfare recipients how to get a job. I was inspired by the power of nonprofits to make change, and I went to law school to learn how to establish and run my own nonprofit to create change more quickly in Detroit. Fresh out of law school, and after a short stint as a law clerk for a federal judge, I cofounded Think Detroit with Dan Varner, a good friend and classmate. Our mission was to build character in young people through sports. We served five thousand kids annually and won praises from the White House before merging with the Detroit Police Athletic League in 2006. We now serve fourteen thousand young people annually and will soon have our headquarters and brand-new fields on the site of the old Tiger Stadium.

While I was leading Think Detroit, Detroit's mayor appointed me to serve on the board of Detroit Public Schools. I was horrified by how dangerous our neighborhood high schools had become. Convinced that the best thing for Detroit's young people was to start a new school system free of a hundred or so years of rules, regulations and an overpowering sense of hopelessness, I left Think Detroit to help lead one of the pioneering schools in Detroit's fledgling charter school movement. Our first senior class in 2007 graduated 93 percent of the freshmen from four years earlier, shattering the district's rate of 58 percent and all of the justifications for the status quo along with it. All we needed were more charter schools, I thought—but the leaders of the most promising charter school networks in the nation had no interest in coming to Detroit, despite some of the most supportive laws in the nation to expand charter schools, because the environment was simply too difficult for them, and remains so to this day.

With funding from the Skillman Foundation in Detroit, I studied which cities were advancing graduation rates most effectively and came to believe that we could best help young people by creating charter school–like conditions—in partnership with unions—by giving great leaders more control of the people and programs in their building, similar to the New York City playbook of more autonomy, transparency, and accountability. The paper I wrote for Skillman became the working plan for Detroit's superintendent to turn around the neighborhood high schools until she was fired shortly after putting it to work in late 2008. By that time I had taken a position as a vice president of educational preparedness at Detroit's United Way, and we committed to seeing the plan through. Over the next seven years we worked in close partnership with fifteen high schools in Detroit and seven surrounding districts to help turn around schools that had been labeled "dropout factories" by national scholars for consistently having more than 40 percent of their freshmen leave school before their senior year.

In that time I discovered that great leaders and great teachers cannot change the culture of a school by themselves. Even in the best neighborhood high schools, which now feature inspirational principals and idealistic young Teach For America teachers working alongside passionate veteran teachers, they are simply outflanked by the vexing effects of the poverty that surrounds and pervades the daily life of their students. Great leaders and great teachers are critical, but they alone do not create enough breakthrough velocity for young people to escape the gravitational pull of poverty.[1]

I didn't believe that when I began leading the turnaround effort at Detroit's toughest high schools. I learned it in part through my friendship with Keyvon Batchelor, who entered the ninth grade at Cody High School in 2009, the year our turnaround effort began there. In the years since, he repeatedly has shown me the foolishness of relying on schools alone for providing what young people need. Through our friendship I have witnessed the harshness of a life of poverty in deeper and more personal ways than I ever experienced before. I share his story in brief vignettes between the chapters of this book because he repeatedly forced me to rethink my assumptions and deeply held convictions. He forced me to see how much more than schools alone is needed for young people to break through the gravitational pull of poverty.

I have come to see that this is where the church can help, and it has begun to in cities across America. I have also come to understand that when God told me "you can do something about this," he wasn't talking to me alone. No matter where I go, I run into people with a burden to do something meaningful in America's cities. The purpose of this book is to provide practical pathways for how you and your church or your company can do this in a way that changes the trajectory of young people, their friends and family, and the schools they attend.

Meeting Keyvon

In the spring of 2009, US Secretary of Education Arne Duncan came to a United Way conference in Detroit and called the city "ground zero for education reform." I was working for the United Way in Detroit then, leading a network of high schools committed to turning around their culture and graduation rates. A year after Duncan's call to action, one of his key staff members returned to Detroit for a symposium we were hosting on the changes being made in our partner schools, including Cody High School, which had been restructured over the year from one large high school into three smaller ones in the same building.

The day before the symposium, I met with a group of students who would be speaking on a panel about their experience at Cody. Johnathon Matthews, the affable, gregarious, and charmingly handsome principal of the Academy of Public Leadership at Cody, who can't seem to talk without smiling at the same time, handpicked the kids for me. It was the Monday after a week-long winter break, which seemed inconsequential to me at the time.

"Mike," he said, "you're going to want to pay attention to Keyvon. He had a bad time at home over break and is in a pretty bad mood today. He's a good kid, though. Now, he's got a story."

The way Matthews smiled when he talked, I wasn't sure what to think. He said it as though I should be scared, but he just kept smiling. Little did I know how much Keyvon's story would affect me. And in hindsight I give Matthews a ton of credit. Keyvon is exactly the type of student that most educators ignore or hide. They do not put them in front of funders and US Department of Education leaders, especially on a bad day. And today was a really bad day for Keyvon.

A handful of students filled the makeshift meeting room along with Keyvon. We were sitting in desks arranged in a circle, like a large conference table. As I asked the students to tell me about themselves and their experiences, Keyvon began punctuating their responses with his own colorful commentary.

"W' da f—?" he said under his breath after the first student spoke. Everyone acted like they didn't hear it, including me. I asked another student the same question, and his response was interrupted by Keyvon, a little bit louder this time.

"Don't nobody give a s— about this s—," he responded to one young man's earnest answer. Another young man sitting next to Keyvon had enough gumption to encourage him to cool out. The rest of his peers all looked a little bit scared. Keyvon wasn't necessarily a big kid. I had a couple inches on him and at least twenty pounds, but he had the cold stare, inscrutable tattoos on his arms, and enough scars on his face to make it clear that he could fight. I was still ignoring him, not sure what to do next and hoping that he would run out of steam. He didn't.

When Keyvon interrupted the next student, I found myself responding before I knew what I was saying. It's a problem I often have; words come out of my mouth before they get to my brain.

"If you want to talk, you can talk, but you need to cut out this cussing," I said.

"F— you," he replied. "I've been fighting grown men my whole life. If you want to go, let's go." Keyvon started to rise, indicating his desire to finish this with his fists right there and then.

"Look," I said. "I understand you're upset, but . . ."

"You don't know nothin' about me," Keyvon cut me off. "So don't go all acting like you think you do. You don't know what it's like to know that the only reason you were born is so that your momma could get a check. That's what I know. And you couldn't handle nothin' like that, so don't go talking like you understand me. That's some b—s—."

I was floored by the raw pain in his voice. How damaging it must have been for him to believe that he was only born so his mother could get a welfare check. He had been home for the last week with his mother, and this is one of the things she must have said to him in an argument. I have witnessed and heard about plenty of cruel comments directed at children, but this was one I had not heard yet. As I was contemplating my next move, a teenage girl with a stud pierced through her upper lip jumped in to my defense.

"You don't know what it feels like to get raped by your own uncle," she said. "And don't nobody want to believe you when you tell 'em what happened. You couldn't handle that. I know how that feels. Don't go around here acting like you the only one who got problems. You couldn't handle the problems I got. So why don't you just be quiet for a minute and let the man speak."

1

Alone in the Wilderness

Our nation's cities are filled with abandoned and terrified young people. They can look like outcasts and outlaws when you see them in the media or on the streets, but they are actually scared young people living on the fringe and fighting for their lives almost every day. In many ways they are like David facing Goliath over and over again. This huge giant is standing on the hill taunting them, bullying them, telling them that they are not good enough to overcome him. The giant in their life is trauma, plain and simple. It springs from many sources: extreme poverty, parental abandonment, the murder of family members and close friends, rape, racism, hunger, physical abuse, chronic unemployment all around them, unstable and substandard housing, neglect, and emotional abuse. Neighborhood schools in communities of concentrated poverty are filled with children who are facing one or more of these traumatic events every day. This is the world in which many of our nation's children go to school, almost as if they are ravaged refugees. But they are in fact young people in urban America, anonymous souls who generally receive more contempt than compassion, going to school just miles away from the nicest and most affluent places to live in the world.

THE IMPACT OF DROPOUT FACTORIES

In 2007, Robert Balfanz, a research professor at Johns Hopkins University, published a list of 1,642 high schools in America in which the senior class was less than 60 percent the size of the freshmen class for three or more years straight.[1] He also labeled these high schools as "dropout factories"—meaning that if the schools were built to produce dropouts they would have been built just like this. Every one of the twenty neighborhood high schools in Detroit was on the list.

Three years earlier I was on the school board for Detroit Public Schools and one of the first things I did was visit neighborhood high schools. At that time I was thirty-three and had lived my whole life in Detroit. Still, I was devastated by what I found in our neighborhood schools.

The first school I went to was Chadsey High School on the city's southwest side. It was near the end of the school day, and a large group of students had assembled in front of the school. As soon as I got out of my car, I could feel the buzz in the air that something was about to go down. Sure enough, some cuss words, a slap, and shouts punctuated the cool winter air, and within moments a crazed girl had grabbed a broken car muffler lying on the side of the road and was chasing her terrified tormentor down the street with it. I managed to run her down and break it up.

A week later I was at a high school on the city's east side. I struck up a conversation with a couple guys walking down the hall. As we walked, the student next to me got pelted in the back of the head by an empty soda can for no reason that I could see, other than for being nice to me. He took off after the kid who threw it, and I had to chase them down and separate them. This wasn't a friendly game of horseplay. It felt more like Armageddon. No adults. No rules. Every kid for himself, and don't get caught being soft.

I ducked into an "art class" and found some students hanging out. (I put art class in quotations because there was no instruction or drawing going on.) When I asked them about what their teachers are like, they laughed at me. "Man, these teachers don't care about us."

"But some of them must," I protested.

"Man, some of them sell us weed," they responded.

Certainly, it couldn't be so.

When I repeated this allegation personally to the principal a bit later in his office, he was less than shocked, "It is true," he told me, "that some of our teachers do have substance abuse problems."

This principal looked like a smart guy. Certainly he wasn't malevolent. But as I stared at him in disbelief I saw that I was just talking to a mannequin, a person filling a position as leader of the school while his heart had been taken out of him along the way. He was more interested in defending an unconscionable status quo than in fighting for his students.

I kept visiting high schools and saw the same thing time and again. I witnessed a fight flare up in all but one of the ten high schools I visited. In those schools groups of kids wandered the halls with adults nowhere in sight. These schools had compassionate, dedicated teachers giving their best every class period every day despite the chaos in the halls and streets surrounding them, but they also had teachers in some classrooms reading the paper or doing crosswords while students joked among themselves. When I asked what class this was or what they were doing, I was invariably told that the teacher was a substitute or that they were "studying" for a test the next day.

At Redford High School an assistant principal gave me a tour of the building and said, "We know we have trouble with sex, drugs and gambling on this wing, but the building's so big and the staff is so small there is nothing we can do about it."

In schools like this, unloved children who have been suspended and have no place to go during the day try to sneak back into school. They are met by stone-faced security guards and administrators who physically prevent them from coming in. Sometimes they end up cuffing these scrawny kids and walking them out like criminals. Sometimes they give them another suspension for coming to school while on suspension. It can all seem surreal.

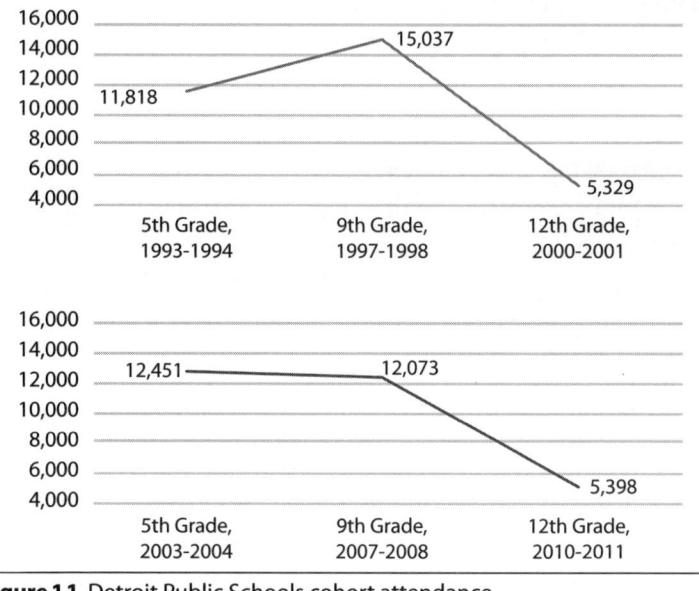

Figure 1.1. Detroit Public Schools cohort attendance

Source: US Department of Education, National Center for Education Statistics, Common Core of Data (CCD).

A PROBLEM A LONG TIME IN THE MAKING

Since at least 1997, and for perhaps twenty or more years before that, the senior class of Detroit Public Schools was less than 40 percent the size of the freshmen class from four years before. Figure 1.1 provides a more explicit understanding of what that looks like, tracking the cohort of students as they progressed through Detroit Public Schools starting in 1993 and in 2003.

This means that only 45 percent of the children who entered Detroit Public Schools as fifth graders in 1993 were still in school as seniors in 2001, and that trend hadn't changed ten years later. Certainly, some kids moved out of the district in that time, but that does not explain why the drop-off is so dramatic after the ninth grade while remaining consistent for the nine years before that.

I used to raise this point while serving on Detroit's school board. We had many presentations on the district's efforts to re- cruit kids away from the growing charter school movement, and I argued that it's not that kids aren't coming to school. We were simply kicking them out. At the time I pointed to our statistics as having 13,000 freshmen, 8,000 sophomores, 7,000 juniors and 6,000 seniors enrolled. When I made that point in public meetings, staff members would corner me afterwards and ad- monish me that the district's official graduation rate was 89 percent. That's because the way graduation rates were measured in Michigan in 2003 was by counting the number of students who graduated and dividing it by the number who entered the school year as seniors nine months earlier. Policy-makers in Michigan as well as most states around the country were success- fully concealing a brutal fact about the number of students being pushed and pulled out of high school in urban communities.

One of the reasons the number of dropouts was so high in Michigan was because our state actually encouraged failing kids to drop out. As a state we concluded that it was better for schools to serve kids who wanted to be there or had a parent who wanted them there than to force schools to serve reluctant, recalcitrant, or just plain failing students. We codified this belief by giving kids permission to walk out of school for good at any point and for any reason after they turned sixteen. Over a generation, more than half the students in Detroit Public Schools heard the message and responded in kind by dropping out sometime during their second year in high school.

Abandoning high school at sixteen may seem irrational, but I think most kids made a pretty rational decision, considering their circumstance. Freshmen algebra classes were and still are filled with students who can't figure out that x is 7 in $9x = 63$. It's not that they can't grasp what a variable is. It's that in third or fourth grade no one spent hours with them going over flashcards to get their multiplication tables down. After getting a couple of days behind in the first few weeks of algebra, they end up failing it, only to take it again in summer school and fail it one more time. They start their second year of high school still needing to pass Algebra 1, but they don't have the discipline or somebody in their lives who will help them get their math facts right. And this is just in algebra. The same goes for trying to write well in English without knowing the parts of speech, for trying to pass high school science while reading at the third grade level, or for needing to be on time every day without having somebody at home to help them get to school on time. As a state, we made a decision that it was better for these kids to silently slip into the streets when they turned sixteen, and our young people consistently agreed.

CUTTHROAT RESULTS

"I'll never forget what an administrator told me after he took us on a trip to Noble Street Schools," recalls Johnathon Matthews, principal of the Academy of Public Leadership at Cody High. Noble

Street is an exceptional network of charter high schools in Chicago. Their students achieve excellent academic results, based in part on adherence to a strict code of conduct with zealous enforcement of infractions for things as minor as chewing gum or going to class with untied shoes. The Detroit administrator who took Matthews and other Detroit principals on the trip was a former charter school leader who had been brought in to Detroit Public Schools to offer radical solutions for its high school failures.

Matthews explains, "We were walking through the airport on the way home, and I told him I could get the same results as Noble, but it would require me to kick out 60 percent of our kids. He stopped me and said, 'Johnathon, think about it; how many students are you actually really educating now? Ten percent? Fifteen percent? If you were to do this, wouldn't you be doubling, or even tripling your results?'"

Whether that advice sounds shocking, or downright practical, the net result is the same: It increases the number of children in poverty. Putting "bad kids" out may be an effective school-improvement strategy for an elite charter or application school, but it becomes a poverty multiplier when every school does it.

"I visited Ethiopia once," Matthews recalls, "and I remember thinking how broken their education system was. They only educate like the top 10 percent—and then most of those kids move to America. I looked around and thought to myself that this country is never going to change. On the plane ride home, I realized how much our system is like Ethiopia's. The top kids in the city all go to one of our two magnet schools and get a good education—but then they leave the city. And most of the kids in the rest of the high schools don't really get a good education at all."

Matthews discovered this when he was an assistant principal at Mumford High School in Detroit. Reflecting back, Matthews says, "My job was to enforce the suspension lists. We had sixteen hundred kids in the school, and on any given day we would have four hundred of them on suspension. It didn't take me long to realize that kids were not just dropping out of school. We were pushing them out."

In *The New Jim Crow: Mass Incarceration in the Age of Color-blindness*, Michelle Alexander argues that school suspension policies funnel students of color into our criminal justice system, which she compellingly claims is an extension of the Jim Crow laws and our nation's sin of slavery before that. She argues that we have actually created an *"undercaste*—a lower caste of individuals who are permanently barred by law and custom from mainstream society."[2] Consider just a few of the facts she cites:

- In the last thirty years, the number of people in prison in the United States skyrocketed from around 300,000 to more than 2 million.

- We have higher incarceration rates than any country in the world, including countries like China and Iran.

- We now have a higher percentage of our black population in prison than South Africa did at the height of apartheid.

- Three out of four African American men in our nation's capital are likely to serve time in prison at some point in their lives.[3]

Alexander shows how school suspensions and "zero tolerance" expulsions in our urban school systems are two key components in the poverty-to-prison pipeline. Suspensions and expulsions have become the equivalent of "talk to the hand"—a reflexive gesture that tells young people they aren't wanted—which wouldn't be nearly so painful if it weren't the same message they get almost everywhere they look. Children who come to school lacking so much support get even less of it at school, and wind up in prison at unconscionable rates within a few years.

THE NATIONAL RESPONSE AND THE LOCAL IMPACT

At the turn of this century, policymakers across the country pushed a series of initiatives to right this ship. At the federal level an ambitious law was passed in 2001, No Child Left Behind, that required schools and districts to report on how all of their students were doing academically, including subcategories based on race and poverty levels. The philanthropic community jumped in with both feet, led by the Gates Foundation investment of $1 billion in five years to transform urban high schools (before—prematurely, in my opinion—abandoning the movement in 2009). For a state-by-state approach the National Governors Association led a well-coordinated and successful effort to get almost all states to adopt a uniform system for measuring graduation rates that starts with the number of students who enter the school as ninth graders. Huge increases in federal funding were made available to states and school districts that passed laws to allow for more choice and competition among schools, including things like alternative teacher-certification regulations to help spread the growth of Teach For America. The charter school movement, which was slow to touch high schools because of how difficult and expensive that work is, finally started to expand into high school and show pockets of success, most notably the Noble Street Network in Chicago. New York City also led an amazing effort to improve graduation rates across the board in all schools by giving local leaders more autonomy to make decisions at the school level, along with increased accountability for getting results. In Michigan, Governor Jennifer Granholm led a successful effort to increase the mandatory age for schooling to age eighteen in 2010.

So where are we as a nation roughly a decade into the movement to create more choice and competition in our school so that all children will graduate regardless of their academic success, poverty level, or personal trauma in their lives?

Significant progress is being made. Using Detroit as one example, graduation rates in Detroit Public Schools moved from 58 percent in 2007 (the first year data was available under the new formula for calculating rates) to 77 percent in 2015 (the last year data is available at the time of this writing). That's the good news being replicated in cities across America.

A closer look reveals that we have also created an educational landscape that provides good options for children in poverty who have an adult in their lives pushing them and helping them to get to the right school—while simultaneously punishing those children who don't. After a century of being restricted to sending their kids to the neighborhood school, low-income families are now expected to shop for the very best schools for their children, and that has worked well for families who shop at the magnet or application schools in their city, as well as schools of choice in surrounding suburbs, which are open to a limited number of children from the city. When Excellent Schools Detroit analyzed what factors led to the most successful schools, the variable that ranked higher than any other factor—higher than poverty rates— was how far families drove to school. Why? For one of the reasons that Catholic schools do well—they are filled with students whose families have the means or who make the sacrifices to get them there, and that comes with implicit and explicit expectations that they better do well. It's what academic folks call "selection bias."

What about those students who don't have someone at home to get them into the best schools, let alone to get them ready every day? What happens when a student can't make it into or through an application school? At fifteen years old, Keyvon was on his own. His relationship with his mother was so broken that she did not want him in her house, and he did not want to be there. When he could find them, he slept on the couches of friends. No one in his life encouraged, or even really expected, him to go to school. And plenty of people were trying to pull him out. Despite it all, he showed up to school. He rarely made it to school on time. He was quick to fight and to cuss out any teacher that tried to correct him. He could not get into, let alone make it, at an application school.

Over the years I have come to conclude that at least half of the students in high-poverty, general admissions high schools have a home environment much like Keyvon's. By that I mean the home is so broken that students are lacking at least one of the following:

- food, heat, or electricity
- stable living conditions
- expectation of everyday school attendance

These are no longer simply single-parent homes but are often no-parent homes. Worse, many of them are wrecked by issues of mental illness, neglect, substance abuse, physical or emotional abuse, or continuing criminal activity by people in the home.

Certainly, many students don't live this way. They have amazing parents or other family members working hard to survive and help them thrive despite the conditions that surround them. But that doesn't make up for the trauma suffered by kids who don't.

My conclusion that at least half of the children in Detroit's neighborhood high schools come from unstable or unsupportive homes is based on conversations with students, their teachers, and principals. It is supported by a recent report from JP Morgan Chase, which found that almost half of the working-age adults in Detroit did not work at all in the last year.[4] Your city may not have rates this high for the entire city, but large communities throughout every city likely do. The high schools in those communities are most in need of your help.

The neighborhood-based, general admissions high school in these communities have been around for fifty, seventy, or even one hundred years or longer in most cities. When run well, the neighborhood high school is like the Statue of Liberty, saying, "Give me your tired, your poor, / Your huddled masses yearning to breathe free."[5] When run poorly, they continue the system of violence and chaos that already affects their students at home.

My argument is not against application schools or the need for them. They provide a viable option for families who can and do take advantage of them. My point is, the battleground for reversing the trend of poverty lies in the neighborhood high schools (and their feeder schools), and that those schools need an army of people to help their students. The effort to transform urban high schools has resulted in neighborhood high schools filled with inspirational principals, teachers and support staff, and it is still not enough. The negative influences in the culture that surrounds them simply outnumber these troops and outweigh the moral calling of their high expectations.

I believe that urban neighborhood high schools are the ones most in need of help from the church. Other schools in America could benefit from such a partnership, and churches should choose the school, urban or suburban, charter or public, that works best for them. But the biggest gains will come from a purposeful effort to connect churches to the neighborhood high schools least well-served by the education reformers of the day, and there are great examples of this happening at some of the most historically dangerous high schools in cities across the nation, including Cody High School in Detroit.

THE PROOF IS IN THE PUDDING

If great principals and teachers were enough to overcome the pull of poverty, the high schools in a new school district in Detroit, the Education Achievement Authority (EAA), would be thriving now. After receiving $10 million from Eli Broad, an American entrepreneur and philanthropist, Michigan's governor teamed up with the leader of Detroit Public Schools in 2012 to transform Detroit's worst schools. They took over fifteen schools, including six of Detroit's general admissions neighborhood high schools, and created the EAA school system.

The EAA promptly fired almost all of the principals and teachers of the schools. They hired new principals and teamed up with the Harvard School of Education to hire any teacher they desired, including Teach For America corps members or teachers from the old staff, without a union or collective bargaining agreement involved in the process. The corporate players in Detroit were all pressured to donate to the EAA, chipping in an extra $75 million, which enabled the district to move to a year-long school schedule and pay their teachers more for it, inflating their salaries above their peers' salaries in other Detroit schools. In short, the EAA enjoyed a unique opportunity to hire the very best leaders and teachers possible, and they did. If unions, bad principals, and bad teachers are the problem, the EAA should have been a case study for proving so. Instead, they proved the opposite.

In the EAA's first two years their graduation rates dropped 2 percent to an average of 62 percent, while the rates for neighborhood schools that remained in Detroit Public Schools grew by 3 percent to an average of 75 percent. Compare this to the six neighborhood high schools at Cody and Osborn that stayed within Detroit Public Schools. They had all of the traditional problems—legacy debts, more than one hundred years of rules and regulations, a horrible brand name, worn out buildings, and the veteran teachers with union representation that had become the scapegoat for all that's wrong in urban education.

In partnership with the United Way (which I was a part of at the time), their graduation rates soared from 59 percent in 2008 to 76 percent by 2014. Those schools, and Mr. Matthews' school at the Academy of Public Leadership at Cody, in particular, embraced partnerships and programs in a collaborative and thoughtful way to surround their kids with more positive people, opportunities, and messages than they were getting on the streets. In this same period the six high schools in the EAA went from a combined graduation rate of 70 percent in 2008 (when they were still in DPS) to 62 percent in 2014, two years after they had been moved into the EAA. Clearly, getting rid of unions and simply blaming the teachers was not the answer.

TEACHERS' NEEDS FOR REINFORCEMENTS

Policymakers and school leaders who believe that what happens in the classroom is more important than what happens outside of it will continue to hurt kids. They expect every teacher to be a superhero, somehow singlehandedly enticing five different classes of twenty-five or so kids to show up on time every day to be mesmerized and transformed by their passion, compassion, and subject-matter expertise. When this doesn't happen, when students show up angry and hungry and cuss out their classmates or teacher because of what someone else did to them, or when they show up late or not at all, whose fault is that? Putting this responsibility solely on the shoulders of our teachers relegates them to a position where they will never be successful—and that perpetuates the low morale, burnout, and negative impact on students, which is already plaguing one of the world's most beautiful professions.

John Owens enjoyed a successful career in the publishing industry before taking a year to earn a teacher's certificate to make a difference as a teacher in New York's schools. He lasted only a year, receiving an unsatisfactory rating from his principal, who was later removed for committing fraud in the standardized testing process. In his book about that experience, *Confessions of a Bad Teacher: The Shocking Truth from the Front Lines of American Public Education*, he says,

> The teachers I worked with . . . were excellent. Exceptional. I would want them to teach my daughter. The problem was everything around them—from the principal's nutty expectations to the poor, even nonexistent facilities to the lack of people and programs to help the many troubled, needy students. And it's much the same around the country. Teachers are being maligned despite their commitment.[6]

I have come to the same conclusion as Owens. The reforms, budget cuts, and pressures of the last ten years have moved out many teachers who didn't care whether students learned or not. The teachers at Cody are every bit as good as, if not better than, the teachers my own children had in pretty affluent schools around Ann Arbor, Michigan. The only differences are that teachers in urban school districts work in much worse conditions, are rated as failures year after year regardless of what they do, and are generally pilloried as the reason why kids in poverty are not getting a better education.

In the ecosystem of school options that has emerged since the turn of this century, it has become clear that the best way to build a great school is to make it an application school. However, and more importantly, it has also become clear that the best way to decrease the level and impact of poverty in a city is to send reinforcements to the neighborhood high school. This is the frontline of attacking the deepest vestiges of generational poverty, and no safety net lies underneath it for students who don't make it there.

The purpose of this book is to share what has happened at Cody and in other cities around the country in order to help more churches and high schools to do the same. Life in these schools can be nasty and ugly without more help. It can (and often does) feel hopeless. And it will continue to be until people who have abundant hope and a burden on their heart to help start showing up.

Making the Commitment

The day Keyvon challenged me to a fight, I took him out to lunch. We drove a mile south to Warren Road, the dividing line between Detroit and Dearborn, Henry Ford's enclave and the home of Ford Motor Company. The suburb is now home to one of the largest Arabic-speaking populations outside of the Middle East.

In short order, I found myself sitting down to eat a shawarma sandwich with a young man who seemed to hate the world and everyone in it, starting with me. But just sitting down to break bread together changed the dynamics pretty quickly.

When I tried to tell Keyvon that God had a plan for his life, he cut that conversation off immediately, blaspheming God and ridiculing Christians for talking a good game but not backing it up with their walk. I changed course, asking about school and life. I could see that he was funny and smart and hurting.

On the ride back to school, I told him that I would like to stay in relationship with him. I told him that I know he knows a lot more about how to be successful on the streets than I do, but that I know a lot more about how to succeed in school and work than he does. I had this unfounded fear that he would see this as a chance to just get money from me, so I made it clear that this is not about money. I just saw something in him and wanted to help him succeed in life. He agreed to stay in relationship with me.

I visited his school every couple of weeks and found him about half the time I was there, bumping into him in the hallways or seeking him out in class to see how he was doing. We connected as long as he was in the places I was, but I had this insistent voice telling me that I could and should be doing more.

During Christmas break of Keyvon's sophomore year, my wife and I read *The Best Christmas Pageant Ever* to our children. It's about the Herdman kids, six painfully poor and unruly kids with a mischievous, cruel streak in them. Their father left them when they were young, and their mother worked two jobs, leaving them to fend for themselves.

When the Herdmans decide to audition for the school's Christmas pageant, they threaten to beat up anybody who tried out for their parts. As a result, the six siblings got all the best parts as Mary, Joseph, the angel and the three wise men.

The thing is, they had never heard the Nativity story—and they wanted to play the roles the way they would if the same things had happened to them. To the Herdmans the gifts of the three wise men— gold, frankincense, and myrrh—seemed like an insult. That just wouldn't do. Instead, Claude, Leroy, and Ollie Herdman give baby Jesus a ham. Not just any ham—it was the ham that a church had given them so they could have a decent Christmas dinner. They gave that gift away to a kid they had just heard of and barely knew.

Reading this scene to my kids overwhelmed me. My sense of wonder at such a selfless gift was matched by my own sense of shame for what a self-focused life I was leading.

My wife, kids, and I had just finished discussing and writing down our vision and hopes for the New Year. Mine were typical—to get in better shape and do things to help me be better at work and at home. At their core, they were all about me.

As I tried to read aloud the final scene in the story, all I could think about was Keyvon. He had been on my heart a lot since we met. Tears flowed as I read the story to my children and as the Holy Spirit showed me that I could be doing so much more. I had been too busy taking care of me and my own. I knew I could do better than that, so I changed my resolutions to focus on being a real friend and mentor to Keyvon that year. This was the beginning of my own Jonathan experience.

2

The Jonathan Commitment

Like many who turn to the Bible in times of distress, I have long found King David to be an inspiration. If I could just be more like David, the only person in the Bible described as one "who has a heart for God." One of my favorite verses in all of Scripture is when David arrives on the battlefield where Goliath has Saul and the army of Israel cowering in fear. Incensed, David asks, "Who is this uncircumcised Philistine that he should defy the armies of the living God?" (1 Sam 17:26). How many times I have faced giants in my own life, only to remember the indignation of David to remind me that I was fighting today's version of Goliath. And like David, even when I mustered my strength to take on a big challenge, negative voices were all around me, just like his brothers told him to go back to tending the sheep where he belonged. There is never a shortage of people to put you back in your place. But David was having none of that either. Instead of getting off-track responding to his brothers, David asks, "What will be done for the man who kills this Philistine?" For David, it was all about winning the battle and earning the spoils that come with the victory. He did what no soldier could because he did it "in the name of the LORD Almighty, the God of . . . Israel" (v. 45). That fires me up every time I read it.

For most of my adult life I have felt like David going into battles against defenders and propagators of the status quo. When you spend most of your life in the city often described as the most violent, most dangerous city in America, you would think that change would come easy. But in reality, many people are good at fighting to keep things just the way they are, regardless of how dysfunctional and destructive that may be. When I battled with them, David was my inspiration.

What I have come to see is that David had a heart for God, but he still needed a good friend to remind him of who he was in the Lord and to help him achieve his destiny. This is what my wife, my pastor, my closest friends and mentors have done repeatedly for me. This is what Jonathan, the son of King Saul, did for David. This is what you can do for a young person who needs you.

THE JONATHAN COMMITMENT

> While David was at Horesh in the Desert of Ziph, he learned that Saul had come out to take his life. And Saul's son Jonathan went to David at Horesh and helped him find strength in God. "Don't be afraid," he said. "My father Saul will not lay a hand on you. You will be king over Israel, and I will be second to you. Even my father Saul knows this." The two of them made a covenant before the LORD. Then Jonathan went home, but David remained at Horesh. (1 Sam 23:15-18)

By this time in David's life, things should have been easy for him. As a young shepherd he had killed a lion and a bear with his bare hands. The prophet Samuel declared that he would be the next king. He went on to slay Goliath armed with a slingshot and then became a musician in the court of King Saul and found tremendous favor in the king's eyes. He went to war for his nation and fought so successfully that people in the town sang songs about him, "Saul has slain his thousands, and David his tens of thousands" (1 Sam 18:7).

Instead of ascending to the throne, David was running for his life in the wilderness; jealousy gripped the heart of King Saul so badly that he wanted David dead. This is where the amazing action of Jonathan comes in. Since Jonathan's father, Saul, was the first king of Israel, Jonathan could have been the next king. He could have lived the good life, seeking comfort and worldly pleasures while waiting to take over for his dad. There was no reason for him to give this up, let alone to actively work to hand it over to David, but that's exactly what he did. And he changed the course of Israel and our world because of it. If people who love Jesus start acting a little bit more like Jonathan, we too can change our nation.

This is the Jonathan Commitment:

1. going to young people alone in the wilderness

2. encouraging them to remember who they were born to be

3. sticking with them until they get there

This is a personal commitment between two people, but it works best when it starts as an organizational commitment between a school and a church.

In the same way that Jonathan saw and then evoked greatness in David, church leaders can make a commitment to the most challenged schools. They can go to a school struggling to meet its students' needs, a school filled with good people doing all that they can but are still not doing enough, and say, "We will come alongside you to help you achieve your school's mission. We will love your students and help them achieve their destiny." When church leaders do this, they create a pathway for their church members to actively live the gospel and to make a Jonathan Commitment of their own.

Businesses and other organizations can make this commitment too, as companies like General Motors and Ernst and Young already have, and more large universities near urban areas should, like University of Pennsylvania already has.[1] This book includes some of their stories because of their impact and potential for others to follow. However, the greatest promise lies with the church—the people who meet every Sunday to be inspired and equipped to share the love and light of the Lord in this world. Our nation's most troubled schools need them desperately.

This commitment does not have to be made solely to the neighborhood-based high school. It can be made to any school in need, including elementary and middle schools. I have lifted up the general admissions neighborhood-based high school because it is the most challenging part of America's educational landscape. This is where the most help is needed, and it is also the place best left to the church. These are the schools and communities most education reformers and others have given up on. The church, however, is built for eternity. It knows that love always wins as long as people don't give up the fight.

PERSONAL AND CHURCH DEVELOPMENT

Doug Kempton, the pastor of Grace Community Church in Detroit, got his start as a partner at Kinkos. I wish the leaders of all churches and nonprofit organizations would heed the lesson Doug learned while running that shop. He realized that he kept promoting their best front desk staff into management positions—taking them away from the front desk. This created a problem because the company needed to have great customer service to increase its profits. To address this need, Doug required all managers to spend at least 25 percent of their day working the front desk. This put their best people where they were needed most. If only churches and nonprofit organizations did the same. Their most talented and passionate people usually get promotions and responsibilities that take them away from working with people outside of their organization. Instead, they focus inwardly on issues, meetings, and teams inside their four walls. The most important work of serving people is usually left to the least-experienced, least-paid people or to volunteers. And the passion of the leaders diminishes over time, stultified by the minutiae of running an organization, until the organization itself loses its passion too.

"The power of the church in world history is twofold," says Billy Thrall, who pastored a church in Phoenix and now serves in the Arizona state government.

It's the gathered church, but it's also the scattered church. If we are only about the gathered church, we will die.

They built this thing in Arizona called the Biosphere. It was an attempt to create a container for life that they could take to Mars or the Moon. And it didn't go as planned. The plants died. The water got gross, and they realized you have to have external forces on things to keep them alive. Trees fell over inside the Biosphere because they didn't have wind to fight against to make them strong. It's a fascinating study.

The church makes that mistake. We think the role of the church is to incubate, to isolate. Make it safe. Make sure our kids don't get weird by those other kids. We wrongly assume safety and health come from isolation. As a parent, I know this is hard. Being a kid is hard. Being in church is hard. The job of the pastor is tough. Because this stuff matters, and the gathered church matters. But if we only do the gathered piece, we'll die. We'll become irrelevant. We'll become the biosphere. We'll kill each other too, by the way. Suddenly gossip becomes more important than mission.[2]

Making the Jonathan Commitment can change that, not just for your church but for you, whether you are the pastor or a member. And it begins with a willingness to go to where the schools and people are who need you the most.

WILLING TO GO

In America we are living more segregated lives than ever before—not simply based on race but increasingly on educational and income levels as well. In *Coming Apart: The State of White America, 1960-2010*, Charles Murray examines the lifestyle differences between the highest and lowest income levels of white people to explore the ways our country is becoming increasingly divided. He shows that as an increasing number of women began getting college degrees in the 1960s and 1970s, they often married men with college degrees. Over time, these couples chose to live in neighborhoods with other couples like themselves. These communities have grown into "super-zip codes"—Murray's term to describe a bubble of people who live and act much differently than most Americans—over the last forty years. In those forty years the percentage of people with a college degree living in those communities has almost tripled, from 26 percent to 67 percent, and their median income has followed suit, from $84,000 to $163,000. This density of people with college degrees in some communities has created a critical mass that created a culture of their own, and their culture is remarkably removed from mainstream America.[3]

On the other side of the spectrum, young people raised in poverty are more isolated from the mainstream culture than ever before. According to an analysis by the Brookings Institute, the number of people in the United States living in communities of concentrated poverty (in which more than 40 percent of the population lives below the poverty line) rose by 33 percent from 2000 to 2009.[4] These trends adversely impact African American children. White students in America only have a 6 percent chance of attending a high-poverty school, compared to 40 percent of their African American peers. This problem is exacerbated by segregation. Twenty-eight percent of all African American students in America will attend a school that is not only high poverty but also in which at least 90 percent of all students are also African American.[5]

% of adults in each income tier

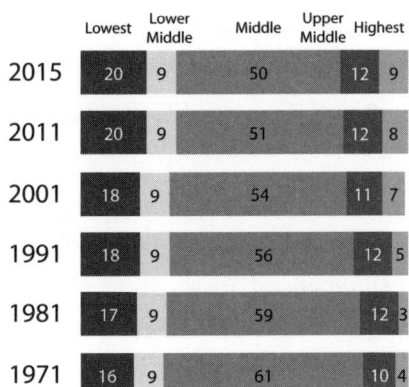

Note: Adults are assigned to income tiers based on their size-adjusted household income in the calendar year prior to the survey year. Figures may not add to 100% due to rounding.

Figure 2.1. The shrinking middle class

Source: Pew Research Center, "The American Middle Class Is Losing Ground," December 2015 (Washington, DC), www.pewsocialtrends.org/files/2015/12/2015-12-09_middle-class _FINAL-report.pdf.

A recent report by the Pew Research Center confirms that the income gap is in fact widening. A shrinking middle class is giving way to more people in the upper-income bracket and the lower-income bracket, as shown in figure 2.1.

How do we bridge this widening gulf between families finding success through education and those mired in poverty? Murray's recommendation at the end of *Coming Apart* is strikingly simple. He observes,

> I am not suggesting that people . . . should sacrifice their self-interest. I just want to accelerate a rediscovery of what that self-interest is. Age-old human wisdom has understood that a life well lived requires engagement with those around us. *A civic Great Awakening . . . can arise in part from the renewed understanding that it can be pleasant to lead a glossy life, but it is ultimately more rewarding—and more fun—to lead a textured life, and to be in the midst of others who are leading textured lives.*[6]

Or as Leigh Anne Tuohy, the spirited mother featured in the hit movie *The Blind Side*, says, "You don't have to look like someone to love them. If I'm not known for anything else in this whole world, I want people to know this—if there's not someone in your social circle who doesn't look like you, then shame on you."[7]

This isn't about the superelite alone, regardless of what color they are. What if we all began to see our identity as incomplete without living more textured lives, without having relationships with people other than the usual bubble we find ourselves in? This is something all people can do. It's what Jesus did all the time, and the lives of his followers should look like his.

For a quick assessment of how far your relationships stretch, look at your LinkedIn profile or those of your closest friends. Do all of the people who endorse your skill sets look and think just like you? If so, you have a lot to gain from your willingness to go. As Murray says, please don't look at building diverse friendships as a sacrifice of your self-interest, but as a rediscovery of what your self-interest is. Nobody wants to be in a relationship with somebody who sees their time with them as a sacrifice.

When I started Think Detroit with Dan Varner, people often told me they admired me for "sacrificing" my legal career, which always made me smile inside at the irony. I lived a balanced life with a wonderful wife and growing family and doing work I loved. Virtually all of my classmates from law school were leading miserable lives, toiling for long hours in law firms that bored them. They had little time to find a spouse or enjoy their family—and I was the one being celebrated for making sacrifices.

When you get out and go, you will find life to be much more real and rewarding. Choosing to go to unfamiliar places and build new friendships will indeed require you to sacrifice some of the daily obsessions that consume you. Instead of serving the god of your inbox all day long, you may end up taking a friend out to lunch based on a still, small voice heard on the way to work. Instead of feeling like you are making some type of sacrifice, you will find that you are actually fulfilling your purpose. All of a sudden, you are serving a special assignment given to you by the Creator of the universe, and that discovery feels better than any to-do list you've completed or any drink or drug you might consume.

For Christians to make a more significant dent in the challenges of those born in the trap of generational poverty, they have to be willing to get beyond the walls of their church and the comfort of building relationships exclusively with people who look like them or have similar educational or income levels (regardless of their color). Like Jonathan, they have to get out of the comforts of their home boundaries. They have to be willing to go.

ENCOURAGING THE DISHEARTENED

When you get to the schools where young people need the most help, you may be shocked and discouraged by what you find. In one school that had recently started a church partnership, four students were killed in a fiery car crash after the driver lost control of the car they were racing on a Saturday night. On Monday morning at school, students watched a graphic video on social media of the car in flames with three of their classmates in the backseat while two others lay on the ground just outside of it. Screams of anguish filled the halls as students wailed and walked out of the school in droves. The same social media site also posted this comment from the driver of the other car in the race:

> ☺☺☺ dum a— n— Tried to race us & f— around n smacked into a pole ☺☺☺☺
>
> learn the road first suchu dum a—[8]

He offered no help or compassion. No remorse or regret. Just a taunt. As awful as this is, it's only a few shades worse than many of the insults, smacks, and humiliating acts that fill the hallways and even some classrooms each day. It's only a shade or two worse than the brawls that flare up outside the school every couple of weeks.

But if you look just beneath the surface, you will find vulnerable, scared, hurt, and trauma-ridden young people who don't want to live that way. They are angry. Angry at the fathers and mothers who left them. Angry at people who have abused them. Angry at classmates who talk so much in class that the teacher can't get control. Angry at the world for their hunger and their lack of sleep. Angry at the chaos that surrounds them. And angry at themselves for being stuck in this rut. There's compelling research that children in this environment suffer from post-traumatic stress disorder, but folks in this work will tell you that it's actually CTSD—*continuing* traumatic stress disorder.[9]

If we rely on what we've always done to help young people, we'll wait for new laws to be put into place telling teachers or principals how to do their job differently. We'll argue that the government should put more money into schools or that people should be better parents. And, of course, we'll get what we've already got.

What young people need most is the change that takes place in their heart through relationships. In his seminal book *The Tipping Point: How Little Things Can Make a Big Difference*, Malcolm Gladwell points out that a few more relationships can have a huge impact.

All epidemics have Tipping Points. Jonathan Crane, a sociologist at the University of Illinois, has looked at the effect the number of role models in a community—the professionals, managers, teachers whom the Census Bureau has defined as "high status"—has on the lives of teenagers in the same neighborhood. He found little difference in pregnancy rates or school drop-out rates in neighborhoods of between 40 and 5 percent of high-status workers. But when the number of professionals dropped below 5 percent, the problems exploded. For black schoolchildren, for example, as the percentage of high-status workers falls just 2.2 percentage points—from 5.6 percent to 3.4 percent—drop-out rates more than double. At the same Tipping Point, the rates of childbearing for teenaged girls—which barely move at all up to that point—nearly double. We assume, intuitively, that neighborhoods and social problems decline in some kind of steady progression. But sometimes they may not decline steadily at all; at the Tipping Point, schools can lose control of their students, and family life can disintegrate all at once.[10]

If the loss of just a few role models in a community can have such a deleterious impact on children, imagine what can happen with an infusion of positive role models in purposeful relationships in those same communities. Something powerful occurs when adults say by their presence (not their words), "I could be anywhere in the world right now, but I'm choosing to be here with you because there's something in you I find valuable." That message, when backed up by consistency and authenticity, breaks through to young people in ways that teachers and principals can't always do on their own. When that statement is made in action by a church to a school, and then made evident every day by the lives of its members, it brings life. It can restore the heart of a school and its students, and that is the essence of what it means to encourage.

STICK WITH THEM

A church's commitment to a school, and your commitment to a young person, should not be based on a timeline. Foundation support and the nonprofit programs they fund usually come with a time limit. When the funds go away, so do the people. Even when the programs are long-lasting, they are typically limited to serving kids until graduation—with the expectation that this will help them get into college and then become successful in life. The reality, however, is quite different. There are now 5.5 million "disconnected youth"—Americans between 16 and 24 who are neither working nor going to school.[11] The percentage of students in the lowest economic quartile who graduated from college barely budged over the last forty years, moving from 6 percent to 9 percent, despite the fact that the percentage of those students who enrolled in college during that same time grew from 28 percent to 45 percent.[12] By making a commitment to students in school today, you can shrink the number of disconnected youth in the future. The key is making a commitment to stick with them.

You likely have within your network and experience many more job opportunities and career ideas than most students could dream of. You can also help them avoid the college-degree-or-bust fallacy that pervades education circles. A huge employment opportunity exists between the low-skilled jobs that surround most high-poverty schools and the high-skilled jobs that require a four-year college degree. These middle skill jobs require some form of technical training after high school in fields like health care, computer technology, and manufacturing. They have starting salaries nearly twice the minimum wage and offer health insurance benefits. Middle skill jobs currently make up almost half of the jobs in US labor force.[13] If you have been working for ten years or more, you likely know a good number of people who could help a young person get a job in this field. Chances are the 5.5 million disconnected youth don't even know these jobs exist, let alone how to get them or someone who can help them to find them.

The traditional pathways for helping people to get involved in young people's lives often do not serve either party well in high-poverty schools. School supply drives, career days, and school clean-up days seem like good ideas. They promise to give something of value with a small commitment of time or money, but they fall short of what students in high-poverty schools need most: relationships. Young people, especially those in high-poverty schools, want to know that someone cares about them, and they need that relationship to last well after the school year is done.

Even those programs focused on relationships, including most traditional mentoring models, are ill-suited for serving young people in the most challenging high schools. They start with a requirement that the mentor dedicate three to five hours each week to the relationship. The relationship is usually brokered by third parties—the school or parent on one side and a case manager for a nonprofit organization on the other. The goal for both parties is for the mentorship to last at least one year, although they would like it to go beyond that, and is focused on short-term goals like improving attendance or grades.[14]

Making a Jonathan Commitment is different in four critical ways:

1. The relationship is *entered into freely* by both people.

2. It *does not have a formal time requirement* other than what is needed to continue a meaningful friendship.

3. It is based on helping one person get to a specific *long-term goal in life*—like marriage, college, or the start of a career—with a much farther horizon than traditional mentoring programs.

4. It is based on *mutual friendship*, where both people are expected to give and to receive.

When I told Keyvon that I wanted to help him be successful in life, I made a Jonathan Commitment. I knew lots of young people at that time, but God had put a special burden on my heart to do something extra for him. There are coaches, teachers, extended family members, and neighbors doing this all the time in low-income communities, but they are not enough. Young people battling to escape poverty need more people like them in their lives, and the church can be the source to bring them there.

When your church becomes a Jonathan to a school, you may be amazed at how many jobs your friends can help young people find. When you become a Jonathan to a young person, you will be thrilled to see them succeed in a job they never would have known about if not for their friendship with you. But again, you have to be willing to stick with them after high school to make this happen.

Becoming
a Dad

When Christmas break ended, I went by the Cody Academy of Public Leadership to make good on my commitment for a real friendship with Keyvon. But it was too late. His mom had put him out of the house. He had stopped coming to school and was living with one of his friends. The school had some addresses and phone numbers on record for him, and I searched for him, leaving notes on the doors of different homes around the city. Still, no luck. Finally I went to his adviser, the incredibly tough and sweet Mrs. Raye, and she got me sorted out immediately.

"His girlfriend goes to MCH"—one of the other two small schools in the building—"I'll get her to have him call you," she said, and was off in search of his girlfriend. Sure enough, my phone rang about five minutes later. I told Keyvon how God had him on my heart, and that I wanted to be there for him. So we agreed to meet at the school a week later at 9 a.m. in Mr. Matthews's office.

The following week Keyvon showed up as promised, but about ten minutes late. Before I could admonish him about the importance of time and punctuality, he apologized, explaining that he had been up all night in the hospital with his girlfriend, who was about to have their baby, and that the buses didn't run on time from the hospital across town to his school.

"Wait, wait, wait," I protested, not wanting to hear about any buses. "Back it up a stop. When is your girlfriend supposed to have her baby?"

"Aw, not until later today," he said. "Things are going real slow."

He may have been cool, but I wasn't. I rushed him into the car to get him back to the hospital. Not wanting to lose an opportunity to make a real connection, I made a quick detour to the Russell Street Deli in Detroit's Eastern Market, a couple miles from the hospital.

I asked Keyvon about his relationship with his own dad. He had never met him and did not know his name. Here he was, sixteen years old and about to be a dad without having any idea what being a dad was like. So over bacon and eggs I told him about my own.

My dad was born in 1933 in his home on the lower east side of Detroit. His parents couldn't afford a doctor, let alone a hospital visit, so he was born in their bed under the care of a midwife who didn't properly remove the placenta after his birth. His mom died a week later from ensuing infections. She was only twenty-three at the time. His dad was left with three children to raise on his own in the depth of the Great Depression.

My dad never talked about his childhood, telling me only that his dad owned a series of small businesses to make a living. But after my dad died in 1996, I learned from his cousins that my dad's father was one of the biggest bookies on the east side. I also learned that he always held it against my dad that his wife died giving birth to him. My dad grew up neglected, and he left for a Catholic seminary at the age of thirteen, hoping to get away from his home as much as to become a priest and a missionary. But health problems in his senior year kept him from being fit enough to travel, so he was kicked out of the seminary after high school. At the age of eighteen, he returned to a home that was never a home and a father who was never a dad to him.

But my dad went on to get his teaching degree and became a great teacher and coach, indeed even a legend over the next thirty-five years at University of Detroit Jesuit High School in Detroit. When I co-founded a nonprofit called Think Detroit the year after he died, it grew exponentially because of his former students who would do anything to help the son of John Tenbusch, the teacher who saved them or a brother or son of theirs during the turbulent days in the 1960s, 1970s, and 1980s in Detroit. To this day I meet people who hear my last name and ask if I'm related to John Tenbusch, the teacher at U of D High who did so much for them. I continue to reap the fruits of seeds my dad sowed twenty years after his death.

The thing about my dad, though, was that he was an even better dad than he was a teacher, despite having such an acrimonious relationship with his own father. He never quite figured out how to be a good husband to my mom; they shared a silent working relationship most of our childhood. But he was an incredible father to my siblings and me. He told and showed me over and over that there was nothing I could do that would keep him from loving me. Through my dad, I felt the unconditional love of God. Regardless of how bad I argued with Dad or how dumb of a thing I did, I knew that he always loved me. That gave me a freedom and a strength to try things that I may not otherwise have, like starting a nonprofit when I was $90,000 in debt with law school loans, or committing the United Way to turning around the region's worst high schools when it had no experience in schools.

"And my dad did all this without having a real dad in his life," I said to Keyvon as we polished off our coffee and eggs, encouraging him that he could do the same for his son. Little did I know how much he would have to do to live up to that commitment. His son, Keyvon Jr., was born two hours later. Keyvon was homeless, unemployed and dropping out of school, but he was committed to being a great dad.

3

The Church Awakening

The founding of America, and the most important things that have happened in it, was led by movements of people inspired by the Holy Spirit. In *The Fourth Great Awakening and the Future of Egalitarianism*, Robert Fogel captures how three religious revivals have led to political reforms in America. At different points in our nation's history, there were clear indications of a movement of people moved by God to live holier, more purposeful lives.

As those movements grew and people grappled with the question of how their thirst for righteousness applied to the world around them, they gradually saw and then challenged the prevailing societal conditions as unacceptable. Their political aims weren't always clear at first; some of them failed, and those that succeeded took decades after the revival to take root. The first revival in the 1730s led to America's independence, the second revival in the 1830s led to the abolition of slavery, and the third revival in the 1920s led to the battle for civil rights and the programs to end poverty.[1]

Fogel shows that a Fourth Great Awakening took place from the mid-1960s through the 1980s, when membership in evangelical churches and movements quadrupled. The political phase that followed this movement of the Holy Spirit has sparked campaigns against abortion, against vulgarity in the media, and against same-sex marriage. All three have failed, and the evangelical church in America is reeling as a result.

In the *The Great Evangelical Recession: Six Factors That Will Crash the American Church . . . and How to Prepare*, John Dickerson points out that evangelicals do not make up 30 to 40 percent of America, as is often reported, but in fact constitute 7 to 9 percent of the people in our country, or roughly 22 million of America's 316 million people.[2] Worse yet, "Of the 3.7 million United States evangelicals who are eighteen to twenty-nine years old, 2.6 million will leave the faith at some point between their eighteenth and twenty-ninth birthdays. That's 260,000 who leave each year. That's 712 who will quit the faith today, another 712 tomorrow, and so forth."[3] While about a third of those people will return to the faith, fully two-thirds will not, based on the best evidence to date.[4]

Is it possible that people are leaving the faith faster in this century because they need their faith to be more relevant, their walk of faith to be more adventure filled, and the fruit of their faith to last longer than the Sunday morning experience that marked the childhoods of their parents in the last century?

Perhaps it's time for people who love the Lord to fight *for* a cause instead of against one. The ultimate expression of the Fourth Great Awakening can be the church's commitment to stand with and fight for children born into poverty.

Throughout all of church history, Christians have stood up for the poorest among us. But in the beginning of the twentieth century, a "great reversal" occurred.[5] Social reformers became increasingly progressive and progressively reliant on government as the solution to poverty. They led the Social Gospel movement, which shifted responsibility for poverty from personal failure to societal failure, and evil was seen not as personal sin but as a sin of society.[6] The solution was for government to increase income levels for the poor. As the focus of those outreach efforts shifted from personal responsibility to governmental obligations, evangelicals began to lose interest. As they saw their beliefs take a back seat to human systems and solutions, they withdrew even more.[7] By the end of the twentieth century the church in America was still providing social services to people in poverty, but it had essentially given up on the idea that it could and should be a force in improving societal conditions for people in poverty.

There are exceptions to this, of course. Over the last thirty years a movement has grown out of the friendships and work of diverse pastors like John Perkins, Wayne Gordon, and Ronald Sider, who started churches in major cities specifically focused on an evangelical gospel message centered on Christian's responsibility to help those in poverty. They encourage their supporters to live in and become a part of the community they hope to see transformed—even when, or especially when, it requires moving one's family from a safe suburban neighborhood to a much more challenged urban one. They hope to bring about reconciliation between people and justice in poorly served communities. This is a heavy commitment, one that many churches and people choose not to make. Still, this movement is filled with inspirational stories of God's grace and transformational power working in these churches and neighborhoods. The writings of these leaders provide great insights for doing urban and suburban partnerships well. Just about every major American city now has at least one church, if not more, within this network of churches under the umbrella of the Christian Community Development Association.[8]

Of course, the church also serves to help people in poverty through its teachings, classes, fellowship, and support for the people who come into its doors. Over the last thirty or forty years many churches and ministries have grown in part by emphasizing the need for people to read, speak, live, and do the Word of God to receive the blessings of God. This has worked well for my family and me, but it is limited to people who hear the calling and are ready to respond to it. When people are not ready to surrender their life to the Lord, they can't get to the rest of the message.

America's cities are filled with people who have *heard* the love of Jesus from his followers but have not *seen* it in them. That's not to say the American church does not know how to show the love of Jesus. In 2006 alone, 2.2 million Americans went on a short-term missions trip, at a total cost of $1.6 billion.[9] Unfortunately, the American church lacks a clear strategy on how to show that same love to those in poverty in its own cities. But that has begun to change.

A MOVEMENT OF CHRIST

Church-school partnerships began in the early 1990s when a principal in a Dallas high school phoned Tony Evans, the pastor of a prominent church in the city, to help him restore order in his school. He thought it would be helpful if his students had more African American men in their lives.

Pastor Evans grew up in Baltimore and witnessed the challenges of poverty firsthand. In 1976 he started a church with his wife, Lois, in the living room of their home in Dallas. Their church, Oak Cliff Bible Fellowship, which started with ten members, now has more than ten thousand members and one hundred ministries. When Pastor Evans got the call from the principal, he sent twelve of the men from Oak Cliff to the school to walk the halls and build relationships with the students. It worked. In fact, it worked so well that other schools asked for help, and church-school partnerships took off in and around Dallas. Oak Cliff now has a full-time staff member in five of the city's high schools. Six hundred people from the church volunteer in those schools and the elementary and middle schools that feed into them.

Oak Cliff's model for church-school partnerships focuses on mentoring and on providing technology and education programs, sports leagues, and support services for families' basic needs to augment what happens in the school day. This builds relationships and opportunities for members of Oak Cliff to invite to their church the people in the school they serve. There they can receive more in-depth support through worship services, spiritual growth classes, and special ministries to youth, singles, or couples, as well as counseling and support groups.

Over the last ten years Pastor Evans has been training churches across the country on the nuts and bolts of building church-school partnerships through a ministry called the Urban Alternative. Bill Collins, a thirty-year executive from Xerox, now retired, leads this work. He is convinced that every school needs a church partnership.

"Most cities are similar," Bill says.

In rural America and urban America, there's poverty. But worse than that, there's family deterioration. That's the spiritual part. I grew up in very bad conditions in the segregated South. But the family was strong enough to overcome that. Most of us graduated from high school and went to college. Over the last fifty years, the family has deteriorated. And the church wasn't consistently working where families spend five days each week—in the schools. This is not about economics or the economy. You can give people money, and they will still be in poverty. But the spiritual side is what gets you out of it.[10]

SPREADING TO SECULAR PLACES

It may be easy to see how such a school-church partnership could fly in the South, in the Bible Belt, or in "red states," but similar partnerships are also taking off in blue states too, most notably in Portland, Oregon, one of the more secular and liberal cities in the nation.

In his inspirational book about the movement of God to work through the churches in Portland on social issues, Kevin Palau describes Portland as a town "where 8,000 citizens cycle naked through the streets to remind the community of the impact of cycling on the environment and traffic. No one bats an eye, not even the police. The mayor simply tells them, 'Be safe out there. Please wear shoes and a helmet.'"[11]

Kevin's dad, Luis Palau, is an international evangelist who, following the model of his friend and mentor Billy Graham, has since the 1970s held huge festivals to lead people to a relationship with Jesus. But by 2007 the Luis Palau Association was looking for ways to better connect with their hometown of Portland in addition to the large-scale festival they were holding on the riverfront that year. They envisioned hundreds of local churches working with corporations and the city government to love and serve Portland better through volunteer efforts, and they launched City Serve with six hundred pastors to achieve that.[12]

The following year the superintendant of Portland's schools asked City Serve to help out Roosevelt High, the district's most troubled high school. When Kip Jacob, the pastor of SouthLake Church, was asked if his church could help with a school cleanup day, he was quick to say yes, as long as his church had sole responsibility for the project. He didn't want his people to feel that somebody else would do the job, and they didn't. "We had about two thousand members," Kip says. "I thought three hundred people might come out—and more than one thousand did. I was surprised by how hungry our people were to show up."[13]

When the day ended, SouthLake's people were eager to do more for the teachers and students they had worked with at Roosevelt. They had felt the Spirit of God moving in their work together and saw how much more could still be done. They met with the school's leadership team and learned that they needed a clothes closet, a place that students and their families could go to for warm clothes in the winter, or just for school or work. They created two closets, one for the students and one for their families, and they completely staffed them and supplied them with volunteers from the church and clothes donated from its members.

SouthLake members started going to sporting events at Roosevelt, and they noticed that the girls basketball team played home games with only a few people in the stands. They changed that pretty much overnight, packing the gym to see the girls play. They started making team meals once a week so their members could build relationships with the players on the teams. The more that SouthLake's members did with the school, the more they wanted to do.

"God has dreams for the young people at Roosevelt High," Kip says. "They were created for a purpose. Our role is to help them achieve those dreams. For our church, we've been given so much. It's time for us to give."

Roosevelt's football program, like the school itself and many of its sports teams, had been failing for years. Young people unengaged in life and in school were inconsistent in sports as well. Others, like Jerome Smith, had too many challenges to make football a priority, despite their love for the game.

Jerome had played football since the sixth grade and was very good at it, but he was struggling to play for the Roosevelt Rough Riders. His father had died from cancer when he was twelve, and his mom had a difficult time raising Jerome and his three older brothers by herself. Before long, he was living with his grandma, sleeping on the couch in her one-bedroom apartment. His living conditions were more difficult because he was also a father. His girlfriend got pregnant in the eighth grade and Jerome became a father at fourteen.

Jerome's girlfriend wasn't in a stable enough living environment to raise their daughter, Anajah, and before long she was placed in foster care. Jerome's grandma brought him to court so his daughter could live with them.

"It was hard because I had a child and wanted to be a child. I had to man up at fifteen," Jerome says.[14]

SouthLake teamed up with Roosevelt in 2008, when Jerome was a junior, and Neil Lomax, one of SouthLake's members, offered to help head coach, Christian Swain, with the football team. In fairness, Neil was not just a member of SouthLake. He also played quarterback for Portland State University, where he set ninety NCAA records, including throwing seven touchdowns in a single quarter, before playing nine years in the NFL, including two Pro Bowls, as quarterback for the Cardinals in St. Louis and Phoenix.

"Neil's a big man on campus around Portland," his friend Jeff Martin says.

He's our only NFL superstar, All-Pro quarterback that is around town. He shows up at every Young Life event, every Athletes in Action, every Fellowship of Christian Athletes event. He's the man. And in everything that he does he's the man. He can't figure out why people can't throw the ball eighty yards on a string, because he can. He can't figure out why everybody else can't do what it takes to succeed. And that's Neil. You have to love that about him or you're not going to love him.[15]

Neil's first day as a coach went a little different than he may have anticipated, at least the way Jerome remembers it.

My junior year when I met Neil, and he came to practice, no one really knew who he was. He kind of came in like, "Oh, they're gonna know who I am. I used to play in the NFL." But no one really used to know who he was. It was funny. We used to joke with him because we could only find one YouTube clip of him. One Tube clip! That's it!

What Neil saw in Jerome and his teammates opened his eyes and his heart. Jerome says, "He saw the hard work I was doing, and saw my dedication. He had never seen that before from his background or where he lives. He's never come across something like that. It kind of inspired him."

A couple of weekends after SouthLake's second service day at Roosevelt, Neil took to the platform at church to talk about the impact coaching at the school had made on him. Neil's friend, Jeff Martin, was in the back of church that day.

Jeff remembers that day well.

So Neil's on the stage, and he says I want to tell the story of my friendship with Jerome Smith. As he is telling his story, the Spirit of God comes over me. I said, "My God, that story can change America." And the reason I thought that is because if Jerome Smith, a 5'6", 140 pound teenager, poor teenager, who is a father, can break Neil Lomax's heart—and a 4x4 couldn't make Neil humble—if Jerome Smith can break Neil Lomax's heart, then anybody's heart can be broken if they understand these stories on a personal level.

Jeff turned the story of Jerome and Neil, as well as the friendship of Roosevelt and SouthLake, into a documentary called *UnDivided*, and that movie fanned the flames of the church-school partnerships that were already flickering across the nation.

TOUCHING DOWN IN DETROIT

After finishing *UnDivided*, Jeff sent a copy to an old friend, Bob Shirock, the pastor of Oak Pointe Church in Novi, Michigan, about fifteen miles northwest of Detroit. Bob has a heart for the city; he was affronted by the October 5, 2009, *Time* magazine cover proclaiming "The Tragedy of Detroit." "When I read the *Time* magazine article about the death of Detroit in 2009, I knew that this was a time for Christians to show who Jesus Christ is," Bob says. "The *Time* magazine article had said, 'The world is watching Detroit with interest to see if it can find a way to rise from the ashes.'" And Bob took that personally, inspiring a movement of five hundred churches in and around Detroit called EACH (Everyone A Chance to Hear) to share who Jesus Christ is. EACH hosts prayer rallies and prayer walks, and supports ministries that increase opportunities for urban and suburban churches to collaborate to share the message of Jesus. But Bob knew the church could do more because of what the church has done.

"In ancient times in Rome," Bob says,

it was always the Christians who showed up in times of plague. Everyone else ran out, and the Christians ran in. And that's all you know about the year 200 or so in Rome. It's the emperor of Rome saying, "These Christians not only take care of their own beggars, they take care of ours."

And I read that and I thought, *You know some day the church in Detroit is literally going to stand before God and answer for what we did during an economic plague, where everybody is running out of the city, people are running for their lives to save their own necks, and God's going to say, "What did you do in the hour that I broke Detroit?"* And I don't want to stand before God and say, "I stayed in my little white church and we got larger screens and better music." I want to say, "We ran and showed to Detroit and to the world that the church is here to help. We are there, in the mess." That's what I want on our record.[16]

Jeff's movie gave Bob a new insight into what the body of Christ could do. Life Remodeled, one of the nonprofit organizations that had grown out of the EACH movement, was already planning a week-long cleanup at the Cody campus and surrounding community in Detroit. After Bob shared the movie with his leadership team, he made a three-year commitment to partner with Cody, a commitment that he quickly changed into a partnership with no end date in mind.

In less than two years after making that commitment, Oak Pointe is making an irrepressible impact at Cody. Their work is coordinated by Kurt Alber, the church's community pastor, who now works out of an office on Cody's campus.

"I think the school has come to see us as people they can depend on and people who are refreshing to them," Kurt says.

"It's hard to work at Cody, and it helps to have a friend who comes alongside to help." Kurt is able to say that because of how many Oak Pointers consistently show up at Cody, not because the church sends Kurt alone. Almost every week Bob talks about something that is happening at the school, or he shows a video of the students, and his members love it. "You have to keep the school in front of your members," Bob says matter-of-factly. And more and more of his people keep getting involved.

On any given day, Kurt says, "Students can see Ron and Doug helping in the STEM lab, Craig and Dave working with the robotics team, Johnna coaching the swim team, or Mary Kay teaching choir and piano while her husband Wayne fixes things at Don Bosco Hall, a few blocks away from the school." They also see Oak Pointe members selling concessions at every home game, mowing the grass of abandoned homes along with people in the neighborhood during the summer, and coming for lunch with seniors and freshmen every other Monday. They hear about them doing things together with students on the weekend, taking them to college orientation, and even helping them move to colleges as far away as Alabama.

Oak Pointe's people are discovering needs and tapping into their passion to make a difference in diverse ways not just at Cody but in the community that surrounds it and the school system that supports it. Saddened by the low reading scores of incoming freshmen, two of Oak Pointe's members met with the principal of the elementary school from which many Cody students come. They discovered that she has an excellent reading program for her struggling readers, but lacks volunteers to meet the demand of their students. One year after Oak Pointe's partnership with Cody, twenty-five of its members now volunteer in Mann Elementary to improve reading proficiency of future Cody students.

Oak Pointe's lead has helped to inspire Rockpointe Church in the northeast suburbs of Detroit, completely unrelated to Oak Pointe on paper but totally connected in their heart for Jesus and the city, to embark on a similar partnership with Osborn High School on the east side of Detroit. As in Dallas, Portland, and cities across America, pastors are seeing how their church can bring the love of Jesus into the schools, and those partnerships are growing in powerful ways.

Oak Pointe is walking alongside Cody's students for the long term, and figuring out how to do it as it goes. Pastor Shirock could have lived a comfortable and convenient existence as the head pastor of an affluent megachurch, but he saw a school and its students struggling to survive in the wilderness and told them he would serve them and stick by them no matter what.

Oak Pointe is not doing this as some form of sacrifice or charity, but because the followers of Christ want the opportunity to live an adventure-filled life for Christ—or what Charles Murray calls a textured life.[17] Partnering with Cody therefore is as good for Oak Pointe as it is for Cody—and that's a good thing, because it makes the partnership more sustainable and keeps parties on both sides on the same level. Nobody is doing something *to* another or *for* another. They are working *with* each other for their mutual growth and development.

This past school year was one of the more contentious ones in Detroit's storied history. Teachers faced payless paydays while their schools went without much-needed maintenance because of the district's looming debts. As the tragedy of the Flint water crises played out throughout the school year, state legislators delayed in coming to the aid of the district, adding to a pervasive feeling among teachers that the state just doesn't care about kids in Detroit. Teachers staged sickouts intermittently during the year to force a response, and students in some schools walked out in solidarity with them.

All of these emotions were felt in the hallways and heard in the conversations at the Cody Academy of Public Leadership, and Johnathon Matthews was curious to see how his students would respond. Instead of walking out, forty of his ninth graders organized a trip to Flint to distribute water instead. To make this trip happen, they had to find out from somebody in Flint how they could help, which they did through their partnership with United Way, and then how to get there, which they accomplished through some vans and drivers from Oak Pointe Church. They are also learning the periodic table in chemistry to understand the impact of lead in water. When Matthews goes to other high schools in Detroit, he is reminded how unique the sense of service is at his school. He says about his own school and students, "There are so many people around that have the heart of a servant that our students develop the same heart."

BE UNDIVIDED

Pastor Kip saw such transformation in both Roosevelt and SouthLake that he started an effort called BeUndivided to team a church up with every public school in America—and the odds are in their favor, with 300,000 churches and 100,000 public schools. Kip says, "You can start looking out and seeing this happen in every city across the country. There are these little fires now. We have twenty cities involved and strong leadership in ten of them." What can happen when that spreads to every city?

UnDivided's filmmaker, Jeff Martin, is seeing this come to life as he travels the country for the nonprofit BeUndivided, inspiring and equipping other churches to serve public schools.

In my view, this is all born out of people getting this idea and then going, "we can do that, and we can do it better." What is going on in Detroit is so huge. I mean, I tell everybody. I'm not telling about what we're doing at Roosevelt any more. That's the old story. The new story is what you guys are doing in Detroit, what Billy Thrall is doing in Phoenix, what Jeff Krieser is doing in Sacramento, what Chris Gough is doing in Seattle, what people are starting to do in Memphis, New York City, New Jersey. There's beautiful, brilliant work going on.

In Portland, Roosevelt High School has had a thriving partnership with SouthLake for eight years. The church's members engaged the companies where they work, like Nike, to help build a premier football field and world-class track. But not just the sports teams have experienced success. Standardized test scores and graduation rates are up too. The superintendent of Portland has called for a partnership like this for every school in the district, and SouthLake is handing over the bulk of the partnership work to churches local to the school and is looking for a school closer to the church to start serving.

As for Jerome Smith? He got a job at Nike while in high school through a friendship with another Roosevelt supporter, Mike Bergman, who, like Neil, remains friends with Jerome to this day. Jerome is currently working in sales as a specialist at Apple and also attends barber school to make more money on the side. He is still living with Anajah in a home that Neil helped him get, only now he is also living with his girlfriend, Katie, and their one-month-old son, Xi'ohn. Anajah is in second grade and is doing well in school. "She got an award today for being one of the best writers in the school," Jerome tells me. "She already has a couple of awards, and I'm building up money for her college."

When your church becomes like Jonathan to a school, the students in it will begin to develop the same heart as your members, whether that means serving water in Flint or expecting their children to go to college, even when that wasn't expected of them.

That's the Jonathan Effect.

Graduating

Keyvon struggled through school and life the next couple of years. I got him a job with my friend at Russell Street Deli, where we first had breakfast together, but he got fired after a few months for wanting to fight a manager who told him too abruptly to carry a bucket down to the basement. We kept up our friendship mostly over meals. I would pick him up at school and we'd go to a local Coney Island (the Detroit name for a neighborhood diner) or I'd swing by his house and take him out to breakfast if he wasn't in school. His house consisted of a spare room in a rundown bungalow of his childhood friend Mike, who was about Keyvon's age but had not been to school in years. Mike was about the only white guy left in the entire neighborhood. His family had moved out years ago, but Mike stayed in the home they left behind. Keyvon's room had no dresser, bed, or furniture, just a mattress and a pile of clothes indicating it was his room.

Keyvon did well at school when he was there. Matthews and the teachers enjoyed his sense of humor and his earnestness. They also respected the fact that he stopped fighting, never joined a gang and didn't sell drugs. They knew he was on his own and that he was a smart kid who did his work when he was in school, but never seemed to be able to catch up on all of the work the he missed when he was out of school.

As spring of his senior year rolled around, Keyvon was three classes short of graduation. At the United Way we made a ten-minute video about the work we had done in partnership with six high schools in Detroit over the previous five years to improve graduation rates. We featured Keyvon in the video and stated at the end of it that he would graduate over the summer—something we really weren't sure would happen but didn't want to admit.

One Monday morning that August, I got a text from Keyvon. It read: "i made it. grad tues at cass. at 10."

This text stated that he had in fact finished all of his requirements and was graduating the next morning in the school district's citywide summer graduation ceremony at its premier high school, Cass Tech. In his own way, Keyvon was also asking for help—he needed a ride— as well as sharing the good news. With the pride of a father, I told him I would pick him up early the next morning—nearly three hours before the ceremony's scheduled start at 10 a.m.—because I had a breakfast meeting Russell Street Deli at 7:30 with the new principal of the school Keyvon had been kicked out of as a freshman.

After dinner that night, I called Keyvon to remind him how early I was going to arrive to make sure he was good with that. He said yes, but told me he did not have dress pants or a belt.

"Don't worry about that," I assured him. "I'll bring you some of mine." I was only a couple of inches taller and wider, and I figured we could make it work.

"Okay, Mike." He trusted me, and hung up.

The next morning as I looked for some pants and a belt that would fit Keyvon, I realized my folly. A couple of inches in height and belt size is actually a big difference on a teenage kid! I drove to Keyvon's dejected about the difference between Keyvon and most graduates I knew, who never doubted that they would graduate from high school. The spring and summer of their senior year is generally spent basking in the glow of their own prom, graduation, and parties. And here is Keyvon, who struggled so hard to accomplish the same, only to arrive at his graduation without a decent pair of pants and a belt.

When I pulled up to his house, I fully expected to find Keyvon still asleep on the couch, a fear reinforced when I didn't hear a sound after a few knocks. But then the door flung open, and Keyvon was standing behind it sporting a pressed shirt and tie to go with his own new pants and a belt—in addition to the happiest smile I have ever seen on him. I couldn't believe my eyes.

We hugged and laughed as we got in the car, and I made a fuss over how good he looked. He told me how Deb Fraser, a central office administrator at Detroit Public Schools, had seen the video featuring him and had a burden on her heart to help him out. She found him through the school, and when she learned the night before, like I did, that he did not have pants or a belt for graduation, she called a friend from her church on the southwest side of Detroit for help. The gentleman ran to Fairlane Town Center at 8 p.m. to get Keyvon a brand-new outfit, and then ran it to his house to make sure it fit before the mall closed.

Citing Detroit's bankruptcy filing and the Trayvon Martin case, Deb told me the next day, "The men in my church are feeling vulnerable. When they heard Keyvon's story, they just wanted to help. They wanted to do something."

So on the morning of his graduation, Keyvon joined me for breakfast with the new principal of a school he had been kicked out of for fighting. We ate at the restaurant where he got his first job before getting fired for fighting. Then we went off to see him do what just about no one in his life ever figured he would accomplish.

4

Starting Steps for Building Church-School Partnerships

When I was at the United Way, I was called into a meeting by Jack Martin, the new leader of Detroit Public Schools, to meet with his cabinet and with Chris Lambert, a man I had never met before. Chris had started Life Remodeled three years earlier to renovate homes, and he wanted to work with Detroit Public Schools to do an extreme makeover of the Cody campus and three hundred city blocks around it. It was a bold vision from an unlikely source.

Chris, a pastor with a doctoral degree, looks like he could be a professional skateboarder. He keeps his dark hair cut close on the sides and high on top, with blond highlights. He grew up in a small town in Indiana. "We had one stoplight, but I'm not sure if it even counted as a stoplight because it was blinking yellow," Chris told me over coffee.[1] He pastored two churches in California and spent a year with his wife assisting a pastor in Uganda and doing community development in a Muslim village in Liberia before being called to Detroit to start a new church.

But Chris is not too big on church as it is commonly expressed today. "I don't think we are supposed to wait inside four walls so that people come to us for 'church,'" Chris says. "I think we are supposed to go out and be the church." He stepped down as pastor of his church to run Life Remodeled full-time, and he is convinced that he has talked to more people about Jesus since then than he did as a pastor.

"I realized that my purpose in life is to live my life like Jesus and do the things that Jesus did, and that's what Life Remodeled is all about," Chris told me.

If you notice, Jesus went to where people were. He didn't wait for them to come to him. And most of the time, he went to people who were hurting, who were sinners. And even though they didn't know who he was, they had an experience with him. And because of that experience, they listened to him when he told them to go forth and do things differently. Think about that, people did things differently because of their experience with him, even though they had no idea who he was.

"Yes," I interjected, "like the woman at the well or the tax collector in the sycamore tree."

"No," he corrected me. "Not just them. I'm talking about his closest friends, the people who had been traveling with him for three years. At the time, they didn't know who he was. But he still sent them out in twos to heal the sick and to cast out demons. And they did that. I think that's what he expects us to do."

And here Chris was, sitting next to me with all of the leaders of Detroit Public Schools, getting their blessing to recruit people to go and do the Lord's work of restoring schools and the devastated neighborhoods around them. Chris didn't just get Mr. Martin's blessing. The mayor of Detroit, the governor of Michigan, and CEOs across the city started signing on to this idea of doing a complete makeover of Cody High School and the homes and neighborhoods surrounding it.

Six months later, in August 2014, more than ten thousand people showed up to volunteer for at least a day during a six-day community makeover. In addition to building a new robotics lab and medical lab at Cody, they renovated the homes of twenty-five students, boarded up 250 abandoned homes, and beautified 300 blocks. This is Keyvon's neighborhood. These are the abandoned homes that he lives in when he can. Three burned-out houses across the street from the school stood for years as a daily reminder of how far the neighborhood had fallen. Those homes were knocked down that week.

Perhaps the most important part of all of this is that it gave Oak Pointe Church an opportunity to start its partnership with Cody. Oak Pointe committed its security team to the project, bought hundreds of lawn mowers and weed whips for the volunteers and the community to use, and hosted a fundraiser. Hundreds of their people gave at least a day of service to the school and community cleanup, which exposed them to the school that their pastor had already made a commitment to serve. One of their church members wrote a $300,000 check to help build a new football field for the school (which had played without a home field for years) and asked that it be called Hope Field.

The following year Life Remodeled led a similar project at Osborn High School on the east side of Detroit, in a neighborhood that had been identified as the most dangerous in the city. Still, 9,500 volunteers came out during the week, removing blight on more than 300 blocks, boarding up 472 abandoned homes, and renovating 21 homes. Donors paid for the installation of a new gym floor, bleachers, and a roof, which alone was valued at almost $2 million and which the school had needed for decades.

Rockpointe Church, whose members had renovated three students' homes, made its own Jonathan Commitment to the school after the project was done, a move that was completely countercultural. The church is located in Sterling Heights, which we used to call Sterile Whites when I was a young man in Detroit. It was one of those predominately white cities that seemed intent on staying that way by pulling over any car with African Americans who drove through it. Located about ten miles due north of Osborn, the city was incorporated a year after the Detroit riots of 1967. It is now home to many of the families who moved out of the neighborhoods around Osborn since then. The church's commitment to a school in the neighborhood that many of its people left behind may be one of the most significant steps toward healing since the riots fifty years earlier.

These are just two churches doing huge things to change the conditions and the culture of the world around them. Churches are uniquely equipped to design and complete projects that other institutions can't. Most churches, but especially larger ones, have retirees, unemployed members, work-from-home members, freelancers, stay-at-home moms and dads, and small business owners who have time to give and a desire to do something meaningful. Churches also have office volunteers or staff who can help to organize large projects, and they have members working in a broad array of industries who can provide professional expertise—and often recruit their company to lend a hand. They have a weekly meeting every Sunday to provide updates and recruit more people, not to mention a biblical mandate to go out and do good works for the glory of God, especially for the fatherless and widows (Mt 5:16; Jas 1:27). No other sector in American society has the depth and breadth of people who can and should help.

Your church does not have to be large, like SouthLake. You don't need to have a colorful presence, like Chris Lambert. You don't need to do something as massive as Life Remodeled.

Take it from Brock Shiffer, a seventy-three-year-old pastor who went to divinity school at the age of fifty-five and pastored his first church at the age of sixty. His church had dwindled to fifty-five or sixty members when a friend flew him to Washington, DC, to see *UnDivided,* and he was mesmerized. "I went home and told the church, point blank, we are changing the direction of this church," Brock says. He reached out to friends at the local military base near in Homestead, Florida, as well as his friends in ministry, to take on six school partnerships in a nine-month period, focused primarily on getting mentors to help students in the third and fourth grade to read at grade level. The schools are starting to move up from getting Fs and Ds on the state's school report card, and Brock has a God-sized dream of inspiring similar partnerships in every school in Dade County, one of the largest school districts in the nation.

What makes this unique is that Brock no longer has a church. He's transitioned from Speedway Church to Speedway Ministries. When I asked him what he needed to know to get started, he said, "The Holy Spirit. I have no training in this whatsoever. When I went out to the airbase and said, 'General, I need some help.' He said, 'Brock, my people are warriors. They won't know what to do.' I said, 'But they know how to talk and how to listen.'"

"When these kids see the men in uniform, they straighten up, and it's 'yes, sir' and 'no, sir.' And the only question they ask at the end is, 'Are you coming back?' There is no other guideline to get started than that: just show up and keep coming back."[2]

If you or your church is considering a partnership with a school, there are some things you can do to start the relationship well and to put the right foundation in place for long-term success.

BEFORE YOU GET STARTED

For the commitment to become a way of life at the church, it must have the heart of the senior pastor and leadership team. Without that, this partnership will wither away instead of becoming a way of life. Before a church makes a Jonathan Commitment to a school, the senior pastor should be prepared to

- Be personally present at the initial meetings with school leadership and at strategic school meetings and events going forward.

- Make time on Sundays for stories, announcements, or speakers from the school, as well as making prominent space available in the church bulletin and on the church website for news about the partnership.

- Commit one full-time staff member or volunteer to the partnership who reports directly to the senior pastor and has a seat on the church's leadership team, and that liaison should spend at least half of their workweek inside of the school. I will refer to this position as the "liaison" for simplicity's sake, but you should use a better title, like community pastor or partnership director.

- Keep this commitment until the school achieves its destiny. This will take at least five years, and likely much longer, but do not start the partnership with a one-year or three-year commitment. That's not a partnership. It's a program. Schools have more than enough programs.

For the commitment to become a way of life in the school, the principal of the school must be prepared to do two things:

- Include the church's liaison on the school's leadership team.
- Give the liaison office space in the school.

Getting a seat at the leadership table in a school can be daunting, for some schools may not have consistent leadership team meetings. If they don't meet regularly, the liaison's first role can be to schedule and facilitate those meetings. If they do meet regularly, they may not be open to having a stranger from a church join them. With so many nonprofits and other partners trying to help the school, why should the church partner receive this special status? Because the church's role is to fill the gaps that no one else can. Having this seat, even if no leadership table exists, must not be compromised. The church's liaison must have consistent time with the leaders of the school to both learn where the church can best help and also to send a message to the teachers and other staff and partners in the building that this relationship is an important one, especially in the early days when it may not be clear what its value will be.

GETTING STARTED

In my walk with God, I have come to think that he rarely does things the same way twice. He spoke to Moses through a burning bush and to Balaam through a donkey. Sometimes I hear his will for me in the middle of the night, other times in worship, and other times through a conversation with my wife, kids, a close friend, or complete stranger. I say this because I think God wants us to rely on him more than on humans. He guides and provides for his people and work in ways that I have not thought of or could imagine. So the following steps are offered as suggestions, not mandates, of what can be helpful in launching church-school partnerships.

STEP 1: PRAY FOR THE RIGHT SCHOOL

Before you do anything else, ask God to show you the school that is meant for you. As you, your church leadership team, or your entire church goes to God in prayer about this, start turning over the soil looking for a fertile place to sow. Read the daily paper with a heart for what is happening in the schools. You may hear about something awesome or awful happening in one that draws you to it. Meet with the school district's central office leadership and ask them for recommendations. They may give you three or four choices with one obvious fit for you. Talk to your members. You may find that someone's niece, nephew, or neighbor is the principal of a school looking for help, or that many of your members attended one high school that needs your church. Don't get the paralysis of analysis here. If you decide that your church should become like Jonathan to a school, it should not take longer than a month or two of prayer and due diligence before you find the right school.

STEP 2: ASK HOW YOU CAN HELP

The last thing you want to do is to tell the school how you will help. This is one of the first lessons that SouthLake Church learned at Roosevelt. They had just completed a massive school cleanup, and their people were fired up to do more. They wanted to start a mentoring program. When they met with the school leadership to discuss this idea, the school's director of community engagement told them that their offer to start a mentoring program was like asking for marriage before the first date.

Kristine Sommer, who led the partnership for SouthLake, explains,

Oftentimes, schools in underserved populations already have programs doing mentoring but are underfunded and anemic. They don't necessarily need another organization telling them we have another program. It feels like more of a burden, sometimes, to the administration than the potential for some help. We love what Jesus did. We call it the Jesus question: "How do you want me to help you?" We know you are the educational expert, and that you know better than anybody else what the needs of your kids are. Give me three areas you could use help, and we will see what we can commit to. We want to help you achieve your goals for your students.[3]

"I have heard more reports of administrators who start to cry when they hear church ask this question," Kristine says, "because it acknowledges the good work they are already doing, it acknowledges their educational expertise, and it provides a path to get further down the road."

When SouthLake asked Roosevelt what its needs were, the first thing they said was a clothes closet. The church was able to establish two clothes closets. All the clothes were donated and volunteers washed and sorted them. They were able to establish a beachhead for students and their families without any financial costs to the church or school, other than the salary of the site coordinator.

"This is really key for churches," Kristine says.

We have to underpromise and overdeliver when we are serving public schools. Because we are not proselytizing, it's our proclamation of who we are as Christ-followers that we follow up what we said we are going to do with excellence.

The most important part of the equation isn't doing what you said you were going to do; it's making sure you are not overpromising. It's the hardest part in a high-needs environment. You want to say yes to everything. But you just can't do everything.

So when you ask the principals where you can plug in, identify one thing you can do well and then blow them away. Because then you can judge how well your congregation steps up, how well your site coordinator is doing. You can start out with something small and gauge how hard or how easy it was, and then go from there.

STEP 3: ESTABLISH A BEACHHEAD

The church-school partnership movement started when twelve men from Oak Cliff walked the halls of a Dallas high school in need of more role models and order in its school. It spread to Portland when SouthLake decided to do a one-day service project. But it solidified there when the church opened the clothes closets. The movement sprouted in Detroit when Oak Pointe teamed up with Life Remodeled to do a week-long makeover of the school and community around it, but it took root when Oak Pointers staffed the concessions stands at every school game—not just the ones at the new football field but other sports like girls basketball too. When the school leaders tell you what they need, keep your ears wide open for a way that your people can have a consistent and visible presence to meet a school's deeply felt need and start building relationships with staff and students. This is the beachhead you want to establish.

At Osborn High School in Detroit, Erika Beal, the liaison from Rockpointe Church, learned in school leadership team meetings that they did not have enough capacity to staff the library. A local company had just donated two carts of laptops to update the library with technology, and without help those computers would either stay locked in the carts or slowly disappear from lack of oversight. Erika sought the support of her church, and their people have begun staffing the library with plans to create a Starbucks-like experience for the students. They volunteered to staff the space so students could come to study in small teams or alone with plenty of adults volunteering to help them out. These solutions put Rockpointe Church in its sweet spot, allowing them to meet a critical need of the school while building relationships with the students.

STEP 4: BUILD PATHWAYS FOR YOUR PEOPLE TO BUILD RELATIONSHIPS

Once your church has a visible and ongoing presence in the school, the liaison should look for opportunities that are relatively easy for church members to commit to while giving them a chance to build relationships with students. In these activities, you are getting a chance to get to know young people personally. Pray about and be open to the invitation to make a Jonathan Commitment to a student who is on your heart.

If there is no opportunity for relationship-building between your people and students, you should not do it. Otherwise, you are doing something for the school or to them, instead of with them. You can tailor many opportunities to make it a "with" instead of a "for." The school may need a dinner made for teachers staying late for parent-teacher conferences or for team meals once a week. Think of ways with the school that students can help prepare or serve the meals instead of just doing it alone. There are many opportunities that you and a school can work together to give its students a chance to build meaningful relationships and real-world experiences with your people. I have highlighted some of them in the section below to give you a sense of the depth and breadth, but you will find many more as your partnership deepens.

THE ENGAGEMENT PYRAMID—FOLLOWING, CONTRIBUTING AND LEADING

It's easy to fall into the trap of thinking all volunteers in a school should be mentors or tutors. Don't make the mistake of thinking that all people who care about a cause can give the same amount of time or only do one type of project to be helpful. A group we worked with at the United Way, called Grassroots Solutions, developed an engagement pyramid to help us keep in mind the distinct levels that people can and do give to a cause they care about. With their permission, I have summarized their levels to describe some of the opportunities and best practices that are available for churches to helps schools and students simultaneously.

Level 1: Following. People who are simply following a cause make up the base of the engagement pyramid. This is where the great majority of people are. People at this level understand and are interested in the cause, but they are not sure yet whether they can do more. Consistently keeping school partnership stories in front of the group from the platform on Sunday and in your church's communication channels is an important way to grow this base and to inspire them to go deeper. This can start out with stories from your liaison or pastor or with videos about some of the things you have done together. But it gets much better when you hear from the students, coaches, or teachers themselves. Providing coffee and donuts after the service for the students and some of your members becomes an opportunity for them to build relationships and for your base of followers to grow in their commitment.

Another way to inspire your base is to invite them to athletic events at the school. A couple from SouthLake personalized this experience by creating sweatshirts that their church members can buy. For every one purchased, they donate two to the students at Roosevelt High. They worked this deal out with the principal beforehand to make sure she supported it (and to make sure the kids would be proud to wear the sweatshirts). SouthLake's members committed to buying enough sweatshirts so that every student in the school got one. Sharing and wearing the same gear helped to forge relationships between church members and students at games, while building a great deal of school pride inside and outside of the school itself. This has proven so helpful that the couple offers the same deal to any church partnering with a school as part of the BeUndivided movement.[4]

You can also organize hour-long school visits to help people get their foot in the door. Invite them for coffee and donuts to hear from the young people about their school and lives. In a tightly choreographed agenda, with lots of room for improvisation, a principal can give a five-minute talk about her vision for the school and its challenges followed up by two or three students sharing their story. This is a fascinating opportunity for young people to cast themselves as the heroes they often are, and often leads to a spontaneous and deeply touching give-and-take between the students and guests over the next twenty minutes. The principal or liaison must end the meeting within an hour (to keep things short and powerful) by casting vision again for what the school and the partnership are trying to accomplish, and sharing some of the gaps in achieving that vision so guests have a chance to go home and think about how they can help.[5]

Level 2: Contributing. The next level of engagement occurs when people decide they want to actively do something to support the cause. People at this level contribute time and financial or social capital to the organization. They are committed to the work, but not ready to take a leadership position. At this level there are many more ways to get people engaged in the lives and work of the students, including:

- *Mock interviews.* Every young person needs interview practice, whether it's for a college recruiter or summer job, and anybody who has ever been on an interview can pretend to be an interviewer. By making a two- or three-hour commitment, much like a career day visit but more relational, a person can be trained in how to do this well, and then interview and give real feedback to four students.

- *Report card conferences.* These are very similar to mock interviews, but are done quarterly after each grading period. You can hear how students are doing, challenge them to do better, and help them to set goals and learn practices that will improve their GPA. When you come back every quarter, it means the world to students.

- *Job shadows.* People in your church can ask their company to host high school students for a half day. Good job-shadow days include group meetings for students to learn about the work of the company, and then the opportunity for them to follow employees around different aspects of their job before concluding with lunch in the cafeteria or a local restaurant.

- *Sports booster clubs.* Your church can create or augment a booster club for the school, especially for teams other than football and basketball. Selling T-shirts, helping with concessions, making team meals, hosting a sports banquet, or recruiting church members and others to go to the games can give your people a fun way to serve the school and connect with its students.

- *A free lunch.* Whether you are doing mock interviews at their school or hosting job shadows at your company, real break-throughs occur in relationships when you break bread to-gether. Plan your day or event so that you can enjoy a meal with some colleagues and some students in your cafeteria or theirs, or a local restaurant that gives a new experience to the young people.

Level 3: Leading. The highest level of engagement is leading. This occurs when people decide that they want to own the ul-timate responsibility for the work that needs to be done. People at this level lead others in carrying out that work. You can count on them to figure out what needs to be done and to be responsible for getting it done in the way that makes the most sense. Some of the activities to engage people at the leading level include:

- *College club advisors.* Most inner-city students will be the first ones in their family to go to college. Your church could support an after-school club that meets once per week helping stu-dents navigate the application process, search for financial aid and scholarships, and master the art of writing a good essay about themselves.

- *Intramural sports.* My brother, Joe Tenbusch, was a master teacher and a leader of great schools in both Chicago and Detroit. One of the keys to his success was starting Warrior Sports—a chance for all students to compete with teachers, other adults, and him in games that take place before school. Students who traditionally showed up late to school began getting to school at 7 a.m. to play on teams in basketball, soccer, and even rugby! A leader in your church can create leagues made up of coaches and players from your church.

• *Citizen teachers.* This concept is based on a middle school model growing in cities across the nation. After school, adults volunteer to teach a subject they are experienced in and passionate about. It's a way for you to share your expertise and passion, and build relationships at the same time. (See citizenschools.org for more information.)

• *Club or team leaders.* Most schools rely on teachers to serve as coordinators or coaches for everything from yearbook to debate to cross country, and many of those opportunities never get off the ground because there aren't enough teachers or others able to do them. Your church will likely have people with experience in many of the cocurricular activities that need leaders.

• *College trip escorts.* A powerful strategy for all inner-city schools forging a college-going culture is to give their students a chance to see what college life is like. People who can give a day to help chaperone field trips to local universities will get to see dreams get launched over the course of the day.

All of these examples have a concrete time commitment, a specific purpose, and opportunities for building relationships with students. Taken together, they are intended to create different on-ramps for the people in your church to make simple entrances into a school and lasting impressions on the students inside of it. They all offer the opportunity for people to bring the Jonathan Effect to life.

FINDING THE RIGHT LIAISON

A great school-church partnership requires a strong liaison to get it rolling. In the first year of the partnership the church liaison must play both the role of a pastor and a connector. Simply being present, walking the hallways and meeting people, listening to their stories and needs, encouraging them and not making commitments your church can't meet are all important ways to build trust and relationships across the campus. At the same time, the liaison should be vigilantly looking for ways to bring the church and its people into the school to fill needs and build relationships with young people. This is a rare combination of qualities; it needs just the right person.

Erika Beal is Rockpointe's liaison to Osborn High and a graduate of the school from twenty-some years earlier. In Erika, Rockpointe found a person who is the same color and from the same neighborhood as the young people she serves. She survived an abusive relationship before getting married to a wonderful man and raising their family together. She and her second husband developed a heart for a young person from the Osborn community more than ten years ago, made a Jonathan Commitment to her, and have helped her get into and through college. Erika was running her own business from her home when Rockpointe asked her to consider this role, and she was ready for a change.

Don't make the mistake of thinking that your church can't commit to this partnership because it doesn't have the perfect candidate, like Erika, for the position. Plenty of people in your church's network can serve this role, ranging from the church's youth pastor to a retiree looking to do something meaningful. If your church is predominately white, you do not have to have a person of color to lead the work. If the person is passionate about the work and comfortable in an environment where they are a minority, their race will not matter. Conversely, if a person is in a position only because of their color skin, or if the person is uncomfortable as a minority, race will matter. People in the school will pick up on either scenario quickly and lose respect for the person and your church.

In many ways, Kurt Alber, the Oak Pointe pastor at Cody High, has nothing in common with the students at Cody. He is a middle-aged white man, a third-generation pastor who was raised in a strict, conservative Baptist community in a small college town in Iowa—so strict that he didn't see one movie during his entire childhood. His first movie came when he and his wife snuck off to see *Lion King* after they had been married a few years.

What makes Kurt connect so well at Cody was the trauma of seeing one of his own sons walk away from a relationship with God for three years as a young teen. This led to run-ins with the police and a debilitating fear in Kurt for his son's life. That's behind them now, but it forged a heart in Kurt to help every parent and child avoid the pain that comes from a life estranged from a loving and living God.

Sometimes, all it takes to find the right person is to start writing up the job description. Kristine Sommer had taken a year off work after spending years working in the children's ministry at SouthLake Church. At the time, SouthLake didn't have a local ministry focus, other than their small groups. They did have an outreach in Nicaragua, however, as they had helped to purchase some land there for missions work and they sent teams from their church on short-term missions there. After taking a year off from work, Kristine was ready to look for a job, so she emailed an executive pastor at the church asking whether he had thought about hiring a mission's person, because she would like to do that. He emailed back immediately, telling her that he was literally in the middle of writing that job description, and that she would be perfect for the job. Two months after that, Pastor Kip made the church's first commitment to do a day of service at

Roosevelt, and Kristine's role shifted from director of missions to director of the Roosevelt Partnership.

THE ROLE OF THE LIAISON

Liaisons should have the heart of a pastor, but they must see their role as more of a connector than a chaplain—connecting the people of their church to the needs of the school and its students. Just as Verizon has set its sights on being America's most reliable network, church liaisons must set their sights on becoming the school's most reliable network of people who love their students and staff, and want to support them however they can.

Take away the people behind the Verizon liaison and he is pretty insignificant. Church liaisons have to see themselves the same way, despite how much they will feel called and pulled to immerse themselves personally in the school and its challenges. The state already funds the school to serve those roles, and foundations support nonprofit organizations to support them with more professional staff. The church can bring consistent volunteer support to be more like family members than paid professionals, and this should be the focus of the church liaison.

This is not to say church liaisons won't be in a position to pastor. When they connect people well to the school, more opportunities will arise for them to serve in this capacity.

"Sometimes, students and staff are blown away by this wide range of things we're doing, and they start asking why. Why are you so giving?" Kurt tells me. I'm curious about his response. Are they asking hypothetically or do they really want to know? Does he simply shake it off, or does he step squarely into the answer?

"It depends on the person and the situation," observes Kurt, "and I let the Holy Spirit lead that. Most times with students, it's as simple as looking them in the eye and saying the reason I do this is because you matter to God. Even if they never hear that from anyone else, I want them to know that they matter. Because they matter to God."

Kurt continues, "With people who are further along, I tell them that God loves us so much he sent his Son for us, and he has plans for us beyond our wildest imagination. The way we experience that is to do the same in our own way, to give to others beyond ourselves. And you do that by deciding to follow God."

Some people have no opportunity to talk about God. "We still encourage them. We love them. If the door opens we will have that conversation. If not, we'll let our good works stand on their own and let the Spirit move in them," Kurt says. "We don't see it as our job to change people. But if they ask, we will be honest about our faith."

Frozen

It was February, and I had not talked with Keyvon since Christmas. His phone had been turned off, and he wasn't living at the same place he used to. Driving into Detroit one morning, I got a call from a number my phone did not recognize. It was Keyvon.

"Keyvon! How you doing, man?" I practically shouted into the phone.

"I'm cold, Mike. Just cold." He said in a flat, almost lifeless voice.

I glanced at the thermometer on my car's dashboard. It was three degrees outside.

"Where you at?" I asked.

"Dub's," he replied. "We got no heat."

Dub didn't have an address, or Keyvon didn't know it. But he knew the street name and a crossroad near it. He was standing outside when I pulled up. His brown skin looked ashen gray. He moved slowly, lifelessly as he sunk into my car.

This winter was one of the worst in Michigan's history. The night before, it was ten degrees below zero for most of the night. It had been bitterly cold for months on end. Cold winters are not like hot summers. You don't get used to weather below zero like you do heat above one hundred.

"Don't worry," I told Keyvon as we drove to my downtown job. "We can get your gas turned back on." I figured Keyvon's friend had failed to pay his heating bill, and that DTE, Detroit's utility company, had cut the utilities to the house.

"I'm cool with DTE," Keyvon replied. "They stole our furnace and water heater."

That statement floored me. It meant that Keyvon's lack of heat wasn't a temporary thing caused by a delinquent utility bill that a few hundred dollars could fix. It meant that burglars had stolen the furnace and hot water tank, which would cost thousands of dollars to replace.

In a city with so many abandoned homes, and so many people without jobs, an entire industry of scrap recycling has emerged in the underground economy. Men routinely break into boarded-up buildings and rip all of the lucrative copper piping out of the walls and all of the heavy metal too. They take it to recycling yards around the city to redeem if for much-needed cash at a rate of just a fraction of a percent of what it will cost to replace it.

The house he was living in was actually Dub's sister's house, Keyvon explained to me, but she had moved out a year earlier. By the time Dub moved in a few months later, the home's heating system was gone.

Left with no other options, Dub and Keyvon were hunkered down there for the winter.

When Keyvon got in my car, I couldn't understand how he was doing it. I knew he wasn't getting public assistance and that he hadn't qualified for unemployment. I also knew he wasn't selling weed on the side because he would have paid his phone bill if he were.

"What're you doing to eat?" I asked.

"Shoveling snow. I can get three Ramen Noodles for a dollar at the dollar store, and a jug of juice for another dollar," he replied. "That'll get me through a couple days."

We went out for breakfast and then he spent the day with me at work. As I was driving him home that night, he said, "It's a good thing me and Dubs been cool since we were kids, because we only got one space heater and one blanket to share."

I wasn't really sure if I believed Keyvon when he said that. Part of me was skeptical that he was pulling at my heartstrings for cash. The other part couldn't really conceive that two kids could make it through the winter with one blanket and one space heater between them.

"Don't worry," I said. "We have this huge space heater from the 1970s. They don't make 'em like this anymore. I'll go get that."

I returned later that night with food, blankets, and the industrial space heater, and found Keyvon just as he had said. He was living in a small home. He and Dub actually had three blankets. But one was hanging in the vestibule, shielding the cold air coming in the front door from the living room. Another was hanging in the hallway to the kitchen. A full-sized mattress with two pillows and one blanket lay in the middle of the living room floor. This was their home, their fortress against the cold. It looked like a makeshift Bedouin tent in the middle of the city. And I felt like I had just walked into an incredibly vulnerable space—two tough but broke young men sharing a blanket and a mattress to keep warm. We made small talk for a minute and I left.

They were alone in the fort battling another long night of temperatures below zero with another month of record cold temperatures to follow.

5

How You Can Change a Life

One challenge confronting people who are wondering whether they can make a difference in somebody's life is the age-old enemy called doubt. *What do I have to offer? Who am I to think I can make a difference?* It can be easy to shirk the calling of God by hiding, like Gideon, behind the belief that we are not good enough to do the job well. But when we choose to follow Christ, he pursues us for the rest of our life, calling us and molding us to be more like him. Those qualities can rub off on young people, and research shows that those qualities are also what could most benefit young people in poverty. A helpful mnemonic device for modeling Christ in your relationship with young people is to share his GIFTs. That means you are consistently checking to see how well you are modeling

- Growth mindset
- Identity and purpose
- Father's or a mother's love
- Trust and forgiveness

These qualities become part of who we are as disciples of Christ. And they are in short supply in communities with a high concentration of poverty. They are not exclusively Christian. People of different faiths or no faith can embody them well, but they are optional for nonbelievers. For those who follow Jesus, these qualities are continually being grafted into their DNA.

SHARING YOUR GIFTS

We know from research that everything we do is contagious. Whether it's big things like exercising, binge drinking, or getting good grades, or little things like smiling or greeting someone kindly, we tend to repeat the behaviors of those around us. In their book *Switch*, Chip and Dan Heath say,

> We all talk about the power of peer pressure, but "pressure" may be overstating the case. Peer "perception" is plenty. In this entire book, you might not find a single statement that is so rigorously supported by empirical research as this one: You are doing things because you see your peers do them. It's not only your body-pierced teen who follows the crowd. It's you, too. Behavior is contagious.[1]

That's good news for followers of Christ: we have an opportunity to influence others by our walk more than our talk.

This is an important point: we tend to lead with our talk, not our walk. I have watched young people bear the unsolicited advice from well-meaning guests in our schools: "Make sure you stay in school" and "Just keep working hard; don't give up." Advice can be helpful, but who we are and how we live will have a bigger impact on those around us than what we say.

Being in relationship means you must be willing to expose yourself. You can't inquire about your friend's life in order to give them advice. You have to be vulnerable and genuine in sharing your own life. Tell stories about your family, your job, and your childhood, but not those you put in your Christmas letter. Talk about the challenges you face, your fears and doubts, and how you overcome them.

You may feel that you don't have anything to offer in a friendship to a young person, especially if you are not from the same neighborhood or background. But who Christ is and what he asks of us is universal, and research shows that those qualities and messages are specifically needed by young people in poverty. That is why I keep the concept of Christ's GIFTs in my back pocket, so to speak. After spending time with Keyvon, I ask myself whether we were able to touch on having a growth mindset, knowing his identity and purpose, sharing a father's love, or showing trust and forgiveness. I don't think Keyvon needs just another friend. Plenty of people like to hang out with him and laugh at his jokes. I try to measure myself as a Christlike friend to him, and this is what I use as a guide.

GROWTH MINDSET

Working with a group of high school students recently, I led them in a goal-setting workshop to start a new year. When I asked them to reflect on how their lives had become better over the previous twelve months, they couldn't think of a thing. This was a group of young people I knew well, and I pressed them to come up with at least one way in which their lives had improved over the course of the year. More bafflement. Finally, Deon blurted out, "I'm alive," and the group enthusiastically supported his opinion. "That's an accomplishment in this neighborhood," another student added to the nods in the room. I kept on them, knowing they had more inside of them, but the only other improvement came from a young man who had moved out of the neighborhood. Again, they all agreed this was a good thing. And that's all they had.

When we started the conversation of setting SMART goals that were both ambitious and realistic, they were stuck again. These were bright young people, but they were pinioned by a belief that things would pretty much be the way they always were. They didn't seem to have a sense that they could in fact make things better. This is what Carol Dweck calls a "fixed mindset."

Dweck has found that the way people view themselves and their potential has a dramatic affect on their lives. People either believe that they have only a limited amount of talent or intelligence (a "fixed mindset") or they believe that they can improve their talents and intelligence (a "growth mindset"). Scientists are actually pretty split about how much people can improve their intelligence, but Dweck makes a convincing argument that people who believe they can improve will indeed improve. One of the most important things we can do for young people stuck in a fixed-mindset world is to help them develop a growth mindset.

Students with a fixed mindset are easy to find. When they don't do well on a test, it's never because they didn't study hard enough. It's because they're "just not good at math" or because their teacher "doesn't know how to teach."[2] According to Dweck, "risk and effort are two things that might reveal your inadequacies and show that you were not up to the task. In fact, it's startling to see the degree to which people with the fixed mindset do not believe in effort."[3]

Students with a growth mindset, however, see failure as a challenge. There must be a better way to approach the next test to help them get a better grade. Maybe it's forming a study group or taking free Khan Academy classes or scheduling time to meet with the teacher, but the consistent factor is that students with a growth mindset work harder or differently to get better results—because they believe they are capable of doing better.

One of the most provocative studies I have read about education centered on this question asked of students, "What grade are you afraid to bring home for fear of punishment?" For Asian students, the answer was anything less than an A-. For white students, the answer was a B-. For African American and Hispanic students, the answer was anything less than a C-.[4] If there's one area in which all kids should have a growth mindset, it is in their ability to earn an A. While that survey of students' fears about "the trouble threshold" is now twenty years old, I have found the results to be depressingly consistent when I ask young people the same question today.

When we become a friend to a young person struggling to get out of poverty, we can help them develop a life-changing habit of setting and achieving goals. Think of the best coach, accountability partner, mentor, or friend you have had and what they did to help you achieve at a higher level than you saw for yourself, and be that Jonathan to your David.

INSPIRING A NEW IDENTITY

One of the biggest challenges to owning a growth mindset is the internal tape recorder that runs through people's minds, telling them that they are a failure. As an icebreaker with some younger students, I asked them what three words their teacher would use to describe them. The first student to respond was a fifth grader with chubby cheeks and a twinkle in his eyes. He put his head down and scrunched his eyes in deep thought for about ten seconds before looking up and saying, "I know! . . . Bad and disrespectful."

His response stunned me because he was such a good-natured and respectful kid. I also assumed all kids would come up with three positive words. The next day, I asked a larger group of students to write down what three words their teachers would use to describe them and what three words someone at home would use to describe them. Of the twenty-three students in the group, ranging from age eight to eighteen, eleven of them reported that people in their home would describe them as lazy, disrespectful or bad. If this is the way we think others feel about us, how does that affect our own sense of worth? How would it affect our everyday decisions?

Identity is the story we tell ourselves about ourselves. It plays such a large role in our life, but we pay so little attention to it. And we do so to our own detriment. Our subconscious judgment about who we are often becomes our conscious decisions about what we do, and those in turn shape who we become.

When Jonathan went out to David in the wilderness, David was running for his life. The first thing Jonathan did was to reaffirm David's identity. "You will be king one day." He didn't offer him trite platitudes, "Don't worry. Keep your head down and keep working. It's all going to work out in the end." No. He virtually took David by the collar and shook him a little bit. "Listen, here, friend. Stop running around here like you are afraid, because you are going to be king."

Disciples of Christ follow a God who makes a habit of changing identities. God turned the father of our faith from Abram to Abraham. He turned Jacob into Israel and Saul into Paul. I don't think he stopped changing people's identity when the last chapter of the Bible was written.

When I was a college freshmen, a professor I really liked asked me what I wanted to be when I graduated. I told him I wasn't sure, and he said, "It doesn't matter. You're going to be successful at whatever you do." I was so caught off-guard by that comment I asked him why he said it. "I can see it in you. That's all. I can tell that you are always successful at what you do." He said this like it was a headline written on my forehead. Let me tell you, that man in that one moment did a work in me that continues to help me to this day. That was almost thirty years ago, and I have been through some wonderful mountaintops and many valleys of disappointment since then, but I always hold on to those words in the moments of my despair. I have been fired not once but twice from great jobs. Both times I didn't even see it coming until after it was done. That means that twice in my life I walked into my job thinking that I was doing great and that life was good, only to have my life turned upside down while meeting with my boss. Twice I have had to come home to my wife and three kids and say to them, "Things at work didn't go so well today." It still hurts me to think about it. And when I woke up in the days and weeks and months that followed, asking what went wrong and what am I going to do, I can still hear Professor Williams telling eighteen-year-old me, "Don't worry. You are going to be successful in life." Man, I hold on to that identity in times when I don't see it or feel it at all.

Young people in high concentrations of poverty have had much of their identity shaped by horrible things said about them or to them. While preaching at a prison, I asked the two hundred men in khaki and orange gear how many of them had heard their mother say to them as a boy, "You are just like your father," knowing she did not mean it as a compliment. I expected to see half the guys raise their hands. Instead, just about every man in the room reflexively put his head down and shook it—the pain of that statement hanging in the air years and decades after it was said.

Even when young people do have all of the love in the world within their home and school, they still have vile words spoken over them in popular music and negative images about them projected in the media all the time.

As followers of Christ we have the gift to speak life-changing words to young people who hear so very little about how precious and how promising they are. We can help them see the world differently and their role in it. Keyvon has always shown a desire to be a great dad to his son despite the many hardships he has endured and the many examples he's seen of fathers who walked away when things got tough. But Keyvon never did. When I told him stories about my own dad and told him repeatedly what a great dad he was, I was reminding him of who he is.

I'm not talking about tossing out clichés here. I'm talking about walking in relationship with the Lord and asking him for a word to share with the people around us. When we are in relationship with young people, and we have the humility to ask God what we should say and then the courage to say it, we will find that we can shape an identity in them as powerful as God did for Saul, as Jonathan did for David, or as Professor Williams did for me. It's what Jesus did for every person he met and continues to do today. We should be doing it for as many as we can.

A FATHER'S OR A MOTHER'S LOVE

Walk into most classrooms today in any urban high school and ask the students how many of them live with their mom and dad. You may find a couple, but the answer is usually one or none. We can act like this is just the way the world is and that we better get used to it, but I have never found a child who has believed this.

My wife, Maritza, was abandoned by her dad as a young child. Her parents and their siblings moved from Puerto Rico to Detroit in the early 1960s to work in the auto plants. Her dad got a job working the line for General Motors and bought a home with his new wife in Pontiac, near the plant. They had six children in the first eight years of marriage, and Maritza was the fourth. When she turned five, her dad left her mother for another woman. In his wake he left a faithful wife who couldn't speak English well, had no work experience in America, and was left alone to raise their six children.

Having abandoned his family, Maritza's dad never looked back. He lived near them in a very small, close-knit Puerto Rican community and continued to work at the same plant with her mother's siblings, but was completely content letting his own wife and kids fall into a very difficult life of poverty without lifting a finger to help them. No phone calls on their birthdays. No Christmas gifts. Nothing.

If ever there were a father who does not deserve the love of his own child, this was it. But Maritza never stopped pursuing a relationship with him. After each of our three children was born, she dressed them up and recruited her sisters to go out to see him in hopes that his heart would turn toward her. Every time she came back dejected. Only after her mom died did their relationship change. We stopped by his house one night after a niece's *quinceañera*, and he lit up like we had been close all of our lives. My kids were nine, ten, and twelve at the time, and they had no idea who he was, but he talked to them like they grew up in his house. We enjoy a decent relationship with him now. But it took more than thirty years to get there; thirty-some years of a daughter's yearning for a relationship that never existed with her father.

That's the natural love and desire of a child. A child, even when she's grown, never stops asking, "Why don't you love me?" of a parent who was not a significant part of her life. The pain of that rejection can cause deep wounds. It's a pain that shoots out at every hint of disrespect or disappointment.

What happens when most of the kids in a classroom, or an entire school, are confronting the same issues, but have no one in their life to help them work through it? That's the issue I ran across when I started work at University Prep High School in Detroit. Doug Ross, their persuasive founder, had promised the families and teachers that their school would graduate 90 percent of the students who entered as freshmen in 2003—despite the fact that citywide graduation rates languished around 45 percent. When I joined the team in 2005, the freshmen had grown into juniors, and that year saw a rash of fights we couldn't seem to stop. It was classic high school drama. The "popular" crowd of athletes and their friends flaunted their popularity a little too much, and a core group of disconnected boys forged a common bond of discontent. Mix in the pursuit of girls and a punch gets thrown. But what should have been a one-and-done fight grew and grew. Facebook hadn't reached the inner city yet, but worse sites like My Space had, and these groups of kids quickly turned into "gangs" taunting and humiliating each other on websites unknown to us at the time. All that we knew was that there was a huge brawl in the gym one day and we couldn't seem to get the fighting to stop, even after day-long hearings, suspensions, and one expulsion.

Finally, one warm spring day, word got out that there was about to be another brawl. Pretty much out of options, we pulled every student we thought might be involved out of class and escorted them all into the band room. That was my idea. I really didn't know what I was going to do with them all once they got there. As the last of the kids was being escorted into the room, Jason Wilson walked by in preparation for his after-school work with kids.

Thank God for Jason. He was a member of the legendary hip-hop group Kaos and Mystro (he was Mystro), which came out of Detroit in the late 1980s. But after his brother was murdered in 1993, Jason walked away from the hip-hop music producer's life and a budding career. Instead, he has dedicated his life to helping young people avoid the traps of a destructive lifestyle through his organization the Yunion. So I asked him to help me avert another brawl at the school between the two gangs of kids now locked in the room next to us.

I'll never forget the change in emotion as Jason walked into the room and asked, "How many of y'all live with your fathers?"

Only one hand went up.

Jason went on, "Look at y'all. Every kid here but James doesn't have his dad at home. You are so angry at your fathers for leaving you, and your unresolved anger causes you to hate each other. How long are you going to keep blaming others for the anger you feel toward your dad?"

He told his own story of the rejection he felt from his dad, and the impact it had on two of his brothers, both now dead. Confronting this pain turned the room into a retreat. Tears were shed, apologies were made, and every kid hugged another before leaving the room that day. We didn't have another fight on that campus, not one, through the rest of the year and the year after that, when 93 percent of the students who entered as freshmen walked across the stage as graduates—an accomplishment that more than doubled the status quo in Detroit's public high schools at that time. And it never would have happened had there not been one man who could reach into the hearts of our young men and tell them that they are loved, even when their own father didn't have the decency or common sense to do so.

The thing is, this school was already doing everything it could for these young men. They went to school in a brand-new building on a college-like campus. They had great principals and teachers totally committed to their success. But they carried anger with them, and they didn't seem to know why or what to do with it. We make a real mistake, and do real damage to young people, when we assume that's just the way the world is. You can say that in theory, but it doesn't sit right with real children in real life. They want to know that they are worth fighting for.

When we throw our hands up in the air and say single-parent families are the new normal, we are tacitly agreeing to the reality that children born to single parents will be four times more likely to grow up in poverty.[5] Worse yet, they are twenty times more likely to suffer physical abuse as a child.[6] Figure 5.1 shows financial impact nationally that marriage has on children.

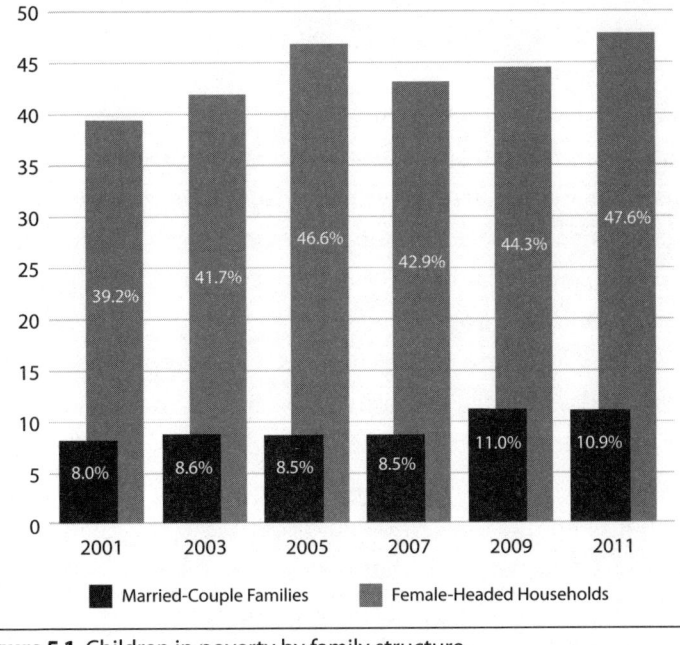

Figure 5.1. Children in poverty by family structure

Source: "The Consequences of Fatherlessness," National Center for Fathering, www.fathers .com/statistics-and-research/the-consequences-of-fatherlessness; U.S. Department of Health and Human Services, "Information on Poverty and Income Statistics," September 12, 2012, https://aspe.hhs.gov/basic-report/information-poverty-and-income-statistics -summary-2012-current-population-survey-data.

Figure 5.2 shows the same impact in Detroit, although you have to look a little harder to see it. The purpose of the chart is to show that a college degree can cut the poverty rate in half for Detroit students, but comparing the poverty rates for married couples with single parents shows that marriage also cuts poverty in half *at every education level.*

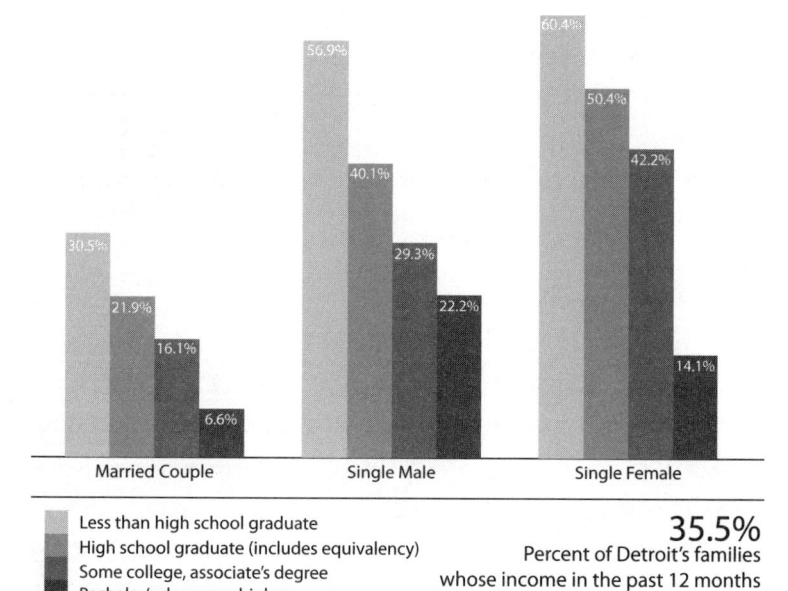

■ Less than high school graduate	**35.5%**
■ High school graduate (includes equivalency)	Percent of Detroit's families
■ Some college, associate's degree	whose income in the past 12 months
■ Bachelor's degree or higher	was below the poverty level.

Figure 5.2. Family poverty rate by educational attainment of householder in 2011

Source: Data Driven Detroit, "State of the Detroit Child, 2012 Report," The Skillman Foundation, 9.

Thus, helping young people get and stay married can have the same impact in reducing the likelihood that their children will grow up in poverty as helping them get a college education. That's why it's so important for us to be beacons of light—living models of what it means to be a good husband and dad or wife and mother—and we can do that most effectively through relationship.

The young people we are in relationship with now will be the next generation of parents, and they need more friends who love being married and love parenting. It's not about bumper stickers or preaching "family values"; it's about being ourselves and living in real relationships with young people, letting them see the challenges and joys of being a loving spouse and parent. Kids are smart. Your parental love for them, combined with the love they see you have for your own family, can't help but create a desire in them for the same. Your marriage and your children are a gift to the world from the Lord. Don't hide them under a bushel or bury them in the confines of your own home. Let the world see your fruit and give glory to God.

TRUST AND FORGIVENESS

When Johnathon Matthews realized that his school was suspending 25 percent of their students on any given day, he developed his own framework to help his teachers move students up in school instead of pushing them out of the building. Just as the state categorized students on one of four levels after giving them standardized tests, he used four similar levels to gauge how kids were doing socially to help them with relevant and appropriate interventions. In his framework:

- Level 1 students have a good GPA and outlook in life.
- Level 2 students struggle in some ways but are heading in the right direction.
- Level 3 students have significant issues with grades, attendance, and behavior.
- Level 4 students are a danger to themselves and to others.

"If you have a school with all ones and twos," Matthews explains, "you'll send your own kids there. You'll send your kids to their sleepovers. But when I came to Cody, they were all threes and fours. The ones and twos were there, but they had to hide or to become friends with threes and fours to protect themselves. We had eight all-state football players when I got here, and six of them didn't graduate. That's just the way it was."[7]

In Matthews's world, "Threes and fours are not citizens. They will not make a contribution to society. Getting them to a two is what makes them a citizen again. And that is what matters. Because we have learned how to turn fours into threes and threes into twos, and, when you do that, you change this city."

Matthews's lever for change is trust—a trust that is built through relationships. "A three has at least one person in this school who believes in them. As long as they have that sponsor then a three can stay." Matthews continues, "A three has learned that he can trust one person, and he commits to him. But a four does not. He will use a mentor." And by *use*, Matthews means to manipulate and use his mentor for his own advantage. That's why Matthews infuses his school with people who can provide relationships for his students from the moment they enter at age thirteen. "When you love students consistently and genuinely, it disarms them," he says.

In his book *Trust: The Social Virtues and the Creation of Prosperity*, Francis Fukuyama points out that different countries have different levels of trust, and those with the highest levels of trust and more of a group orientation have the most prosperity. Trust provides the foundation for increased social capital and spontaneous sociability—the capability to form networks that can lead to personal, business, or community growth. However, the negative impact of the lack of trust is striking in America's inner cities. According to Fukuyama,

The contemporary black underclass in America today represents what is perhaps one of the most thoroughly atomized societies that has existed in human history. It is a culture in which individuals find it extremely difficult to work together for any purpose, from raising children to making money to petitioning city hall.

One of America's preeminent sociologists, William Julius Wilson, describes how this plays out when young African Americans look for a job. In *More Than Just Race: Being Black and Poor in the Inner City*, Wilson expounds on an analysis done by Sandra Smith of 105 African American men and women between the ages of twenty and forty who had no more than a high school diploma and were looking for a job. He observes,

[Smith] found that distrust on the part of black job holders and the defensive individualism typical of black job seekers profoundly affected the use of job referrals in the search for employment. She points out that the neighborhoods of the black poor are "characterized by chronic poverty and a history of exploitation" and tend to feed the inclination to distrust, inhibiting the development of mutually beneficial cooperative relationships such as those that facilitate the job-matching process. The cooperation between job seekers and job holders is thwarted by a lack of mutual trust. Thus, low-skilled black job seekers are frequently unable to use their friendships, acquaintances, and family ties—their informal network—to gain employment. . . . This "go it alone" approach proves enormously self-defeating because employers in low-skilled labor markets rely heavily on personal referrals.[8]

It would seem then that a fundamental strategy for improving the condition of people stuck in generational poverty would be to increase their capacity and desire to trust. But how?

The most obvious answer comes from any person who has ever betrayed someone's trust in a relationship. Trust is built through consistently showing yourself trustworthy. Showing up. Keeping your word. Giving young people a reason to believe that they are important, that you care about them no matter what.

This is the advice Lynn Burdell, a Jonathan friend to many young people in Detroit, gave to a member of an affluent, suburban school board who wanted to help the students at Cody High. Ann Glubinski was at her first meeting with the community partners working to help the staff and students at Cody's small schools. A passionate believer in education and well-connected volunteer from Oak Pointe Church, Ann wanted to jump into the fray in one of our more heated conversations about what needed to be done to make the schools better, but then she pulled back, saying, "I don't know how the kids will look at us coming in from the suburbs . . . "

Lynn cut her off, striking down her concerns, "I don't think these kids care where you come from. They just want to know that you are going to come back. They've had enough people in their lives come and go. You just keep coming back, and they will like you just fine."

It turns out that building trust is actually not that difficult in nurturing relationships. Scientists have identified a hormone in the brain that promotes trust. They named it oxytocin, and they found people with increased levels of oxytocin are more likely to accept the social risks that come through interpersonal interactions. Here's what's so beautiful about that: oxytocin reproduces itself naturally through the interactions that accompany good friendships. Shaking hands, looking into the eyes of another, smiling, or giving a friendly touch on the arm, pat on the back, or a hug all increase oxytocin. And a person with increased levels of oxytocin is more likely to repeat those same trusting and loving behaviors in turn. It's a virtuous cycle in action—provided that there are enough people in a community providing that smiling face, open heart, and friendly touch.[9]

In my relationship with Keyvon, I have tried to help him develop a sense of trust in himself by focusing on short-term and long-term achievable goals, trust in a friend by reaching out to him and looking out for him even when he fails, and trust in others by helping him think through his own networks of people he knows and introducing him to mine to help him land a job.

This is not to say that building a culture of trust is simple. Trusting the wrong person can get a young person robbed, raped, or killed. Young people in high-crime areas have developed a strong defense system against trusting relationships, and for very good reasons. They are also surrounded by so much blight and blunted hopes that trusting the school, the economy, or the American Dream can seem downright foolish. Holding on to that current reality, however, will only give them more of the same.

This is why Johnathon Matthews connects students at level four to an adult they can trust in school to see if they can make the step to level three. And level three kids in solid relationships with caring adults learn to trust and engage and make the step up to level two. Creating this growth-oriented, family-like atmosphere at Cody took eight years. It has not been easy, but it has also reversed decades of decline while similarly situated schools keep doing what they've always done, and keep declining too.

LEGITIMACY THROUGH TRUST

When people can trust the institutions and people around them, they are more likely to engage positively with them. Young people in poverty have learned not to trust the institutions in their lives. The schools and the criminal justice system are two obvious examples, and your church can help to change that.

Over the last twenty years, police departments in cities around the country have reduced homicide rates by building trust in the community. In his book *Don't Shoot: One Man, a Street Fellowship and the End of Violence in Inner-City America*, David M. Kennedy describes the efforts that dramatically reduced violent crime when law-enforcement agencies teamed up with local community leaders to offer gang members real alternatives to a life of crime and real consequences if they continued to shoot at one another. The alternative in many other cities was a stop-and-frisk policy that treats every African American male, especially teenagers, as a potential criminal. There may be a short-term payoff for that approach, but it erodes trust, and that leads to more criminals walking the streets. The reason a no-snitching rule is so prevalent in many communities is not just because young people don't trust the police, it's because they are so angry at them for the way they have been treated for so long, according to Kennedy.[10]

Kennedy describes the key distinction between the approaches as one of legitimacy. Do the actions of the police carry a sense of legitimacy in the eyes of the community? Stop-and-frisk policies in cities, like suspensions and expulsions in schools, generally don't. We keep doing these policies and practices despite the fact that their impact perpetuates the very problem we are trying to improve. A school that surrounds its students with loving adults is one way to create legitimacy—and trust—in the lives of its students.

This sense of legitimacy, of trust in the school in the eyes of the community, is one of the more notable changes at Roosevelt High School in Portland. The process takes time, and it occurs through the collective effects of hundreds and hundreds of experiences, relationships, and events.

One of the people at Roosevelt High School who most disliked the SouthLake partnership was a social worker from a nonfaith background who believed that all Christians have a political agenda. "At first she was really reticent about us being there," Kristine Sommer, the SouthLake liaison, recalls.

She'd been there maybe a year before we got there. She'd been working her rear off to get kids connected to the right resources. She had been working in social services her whole career, so she knew where all the resources were in Portland. If a kid was hungry or homeless, she knew where to refer them. But she didn't have resources at her disposal. She was the one who said we need a clothes closet. She kept asking us, "Why are you doing this? I don't understand. It seems like you guys don't have an agenda." We kept telling her, "Jesus told us to. But we don't have an agenda." It didn't take her too long to see that we were really there to see that kids had warm clothes and to do what we could.

Seven years later, the funding ran out for the social worker's position. Kristine had moved to California a couple years earlier to help lead the BeUndivided work nationally, but the social worker called to assure her that things would be okay at the school. She said, "Before you came, I went to the homecoming game, and there were thirty people there. I went this last fall, and there were 1,500 people there. I know that was because of SouthLake."

Kristine reflects back on the impact, "That first year, those were SouthLake people at the game. This last year, they were mostly people from the community—because energy attracts energy." That is what can happen when trusting relationships are purposely built over years. It doesn't just build trust between people in the school; it builds trust between the community and the school itself.

It may be that the church itself has lost legitimacy in communities with high concentrations of poverty. Many who have heard that Jesus loves them have not seen his love in action. Your church's love for a school and its students could help to change that too.

OFFERING FORGIVENESS

In a relationship, trust and forgiveness are reciprocal. They are like salt and pepper. They must travel across the table together, even if you only want one of them.

Without forgiveness, the offenses pile one on top of another, hanging around and weighing kids down until every slight or perceived offense becomes a trigger to act out or to shut down. This is what young people mean when they say, "I used to be bad." Reflecting back on how they acted in elementary or middle school. They were so angry they got into fights all the time and did not know why.

One question young people often ask when we talk about the need for forgiveness is whether they can forgive somebody who hasn't asked for it. "How can I forgive my father for abandoning me when he ain't even sorry he did it?" This is the challenge that faced my wife, and it may be the hardest thing to do, to forgive somebody who broke your heart and doesn't even seem to care. But to be able to encourage a young person to do this, not for somebody else's sake but for their own, can be a life-changing experience on its own.

In relationships with younger people, a Jonathan friend can serve as a proxy for bringing forgiveness. This is one of the things Matthews does. "When a kid comes to me for a discipline issue, I don't talk to them much about the incident that just happened," he says. "I ask them what's going on, how did they get here? I ask them how long they've been living this way. The other day a student told me he's been smoking weed since he was five years old. When I told him that's not his fault, he began to cry. I told him that the adults in his life have let him down. But what happens now is his responsibility."[11]

Twenty years earlier Matthews was forced to learn the power of forgiveness, even when it's not requested. While studying education at Eastern Michigan University, he was shot walking home with a friend from a party. The bullet went in one side of his abdomen and came out the other, traveling the width of his body. He was in a coma for six days and was forced to take an entire semester off school to recover. He knew what it felt like to be shot for no reason—to be treated as if his life simply did not matter. People around town knew who the shooter was, but no one was courageous enough or cared enough to come forward and say so to the police. Life went on for the shooter as if nothing had ever happened, while Matthews took months to heal. For his own sake, he had to forgive the shooter and the people who could have said something and chose not to—even though none of them ever asked for it.

Like the therapist played by Robin Williams in *Good Will Hunting*, who ends up breaking through Will Hunting's (Matt Damon's character) hardened shell of self-protection, you can be the person who tells a young person in deep pain, "It's not your fault."

When young people experience trauma without anyone around to help them process what they are going through, they can easily fall into the trap of learned helplessness, where all problems seem to be pervasive, persistent, and personal.[12] Forgiveness can be the crowbar that pries open a life of freedom and healthy trust, even after people have proven to be untrustworthy.

For people who want to be like Christ, the desire to give forgiveness and to seek it should be a living and visible part of who we are. He took us where we were, forgave us of our sins, and separated us from them as far as the east from the west. Then he set us on a path for an abundant life. How can we not walk in a way that shows the power of that forgiveness in our daily actions and conversations?

Fired

Keyvon and Dub made it through the long winter. With a friend's
help I was able to find a job for Keyvon at an auto parts factory about
a three-mile walk from his home. He walked there the first week and
was late twice for his 7 a.m. shift before finding a coworker who picked
him up in exchange for gas money. He missed a day about three weeks
in, after he got hit in the head at work and sent home early. He said he
stayed home the next day because his head was still hurting, but he
did not go to the doctor to get a note, so the company recorded it as
an unexcused absence. One month in, and he was out of chances. Any
more lates or absences in the next sixty days, and he was out.

Keyvon lived up to the challenge for the next month. Thanks to the
Earned Income Tax Credit—a tax incentive given to underemployed
people like Keyvon—he picked up a $1,500 check from the gov-
ernment for the job he had been fired from the previous summer and
bought a used car from his mother's boyfriend. He reasoned that the
car would help him get to work and then across town after work to
pick up Keyvon Jr. He also thought he could save up from his job to
get an apartment halfway between the two. His plan was working
well—until he disappeared altogether.

The company called me as the reference person listed on Keyvon's
job application. He had missed three days without a phone call. I immediately feared that he was locked up or worse.

I went to the house where he and Dub had been living. The door
had no lock on it, so I went in and looked around, but there was no
sign of either of them. I checked with people who knew Keyvon, but

no one knew anything. I called my cousin, Steve Walton, who is a captain with the Detroit Police Department, and asked him to run Keyvon's name.

"Let's see," he said, scanning through the police database like he was looking for a book I wanted on Amazon. "Batchelor, Kevin . . . Batchelor, Keyvon. Yep, we got 'em. Picked 'em up last week on an EWOP."

Steve pulled up the police report like the Sunday sports section and paraphrased it for me. "Seems our guys were responding to shots fired when they came across your friend. They saw him run into a house that was trashed, so they picked him up on an EWOP."

EWOP, my cousin explained to me, stands for Entering Without Possession. The police charged Keyvon with it because they figured there was no way he was living in that house since it looked uninhabitable.

"But that's not true," I began arguing as if my cousin were the judge. He is a captain in the police department after all, and I wanted to make Keyvon's case clear. "He lived in that house. He and his friend both did, all winter long."

Nevertheless, I was relieved that the crime was not a crime at all. All we had to do was get Dub's sister to verify that she owned the home.

I drove to the local Metro PCS cell phone provider and paid the $45 to get Keyvon's phone turned back on. About an hour later, I got a text from Keyvon: "Things been bad. Thx for my phone. Lost my job."

When we got together the next day, Keyvon told me what happened, most of which was consistent with the police report. He claimed that there were no shots fired, that he was sitting on the hood of his car because it was a warm summer night when a cop car showed up and started messing with him, and that he never ran.

"The cop explained that the police chief was out policing in the neighborhood too, and that he wanted to see some arrests made. When we didn't have no papers for the house, he told us he was sorry but he was going to have to lock us up."

"But when you got out, why didn't you go back to work?"

"I couldn't. They took my car. My keys was in the house when we got picked up, and these guys saw it happen and just took it." He explained it all as if it were just the natural order of things.

We went over to his company together and begged for his job back. His employer was compassionate, but unmoved. "If you had only called us when you got out of jail, or came to work the next day, I would have made an exception. But you just didn't care. I can't give you a job that you act like you didn't want," she concluded.

When we got into the car, Keyvon slumped down and started to complain—showing me the emotion he hid from his employer. I cut him off. "Why didn't you make your case with her? Why didn't you go back to work the day you got out of jail?"

"You don't understand, Mike. I slept on toilet paper. My blanket: toilet paper. That's all they give you. Toilet paper. I'm locked up, and all I got is one roll of toilet paper. I used it for a bed. It was so cold I couldn't sleep. And the lights was on all night long. Then I get home and my car's gone. I was done."

He had given up. I wanted to tell him how you can't give up, but I didn't think I had the standing. I don't think I could have done what he had done, and we drove home in pained silence. It felt very much like Keyvon's last stop in the poverty-to-prison pipeline.

6

The Plan in Action

All Things Working Together

In 2008 the United Way, the Skillman Foundation and AT&T teamed up with union leaders and Detroit Public Schools with a simple promise: the senior class of 2013 would be at least 80 percent the size of the freshmen class from four years earlier. This is a simple statistic to keep everyone accountable and updated, and it is built on the premise that schools that are safe and engaging should be attracting as many students as they lose. In 2008, the year before our work together began, the retention rate in the old Cody and Osborn high schools (our partner schools in Detroit) was an unconscionable 23 percent, even worse than the district's overall rate of 32 percent. When graduation day came in 2013, the number of seniors still in the small schools was exactly 80 percent of the number of freshmen from four years earlier, much higher than the district's improved rate of 42 percent.[1]

The official state graduation rate grew from an average of 61 percent in 2008 at Cody and Osborn to 79 percent in the small schools that succeeded them in 2013—a seventeen-point gain! New York City's small-school movement has produced an

11 percent increase in graduation rates, with gold standard evaluation data to back it up. We were able to outpace New York's results without having the full support of the schools' own central office.

Once the school proved it could get students to graduation, it had to figure out how to make them more ready for college, a career, and life. This is where the church came in, but in Detroit, it started out with the community and corporate partners.

Figure 6.1. Johnathon Matthews with LaToya Hall-King and Michelle Parker, principals of the small schools at Cody, with their students

COMMUNITY AND CORPORATE KICK STARTERS

At Cody, Charles Small, the leader of a community organization called Don Bosco Hall, was determined to use his center about a mile from the school to advance the goals of the schools, not just to be a place some kids might go to. Located in a closed Catholic school, Don Bosco Hall operates like a retreat center during the day. Cody sends groups of students or sometimes entire grades of them to work at Don Bosco on common needs like leadership development, conflict resolution, or anger management. After school it turns into a mini-YMCA where students can play pickup basketball games or join a myriad of programs, ranging from making music to learning to sew. Once, when I called Johnathon Matthews the night of Christmas break, he was at the center with about 150 students. For most kids, Christmas break means a mad dash home. The fact that so many kids from Cody opted for Don Bosco Hall instead offered us both a grim reminder of how difficult home life is for many of his students. Don Bosco offers them a warm meal and something to do after school with an adult who cares about them, and the kids flood to it. It simultaneously functions as a home away from home and a school away from school.

The corporate sector jumped in next. Deloitte, Ernst & Young and General Motors cleared a runway for Oak Pointe Church to land well and to help students take off. People from these companies began walking the hallways of the schools when fights were likely, but they kept coming, looking to see how they could add the most value. The solution was building purposeful relationships between the students and their teams to help them get into college and thrive.

George Lenyo was one of those early pioneers. He was a partner at Ernst & Young five years earlier when they walked into Cody with College MAP—a program that matches small groups of Ernst & Young employees with a larger group of students to offer monthly workshops on leadership, financial training, and personal mentoring. He was matched with Porscha Taylor, and they hit it off immediately. George saw a tenacity in her that reminded him of himself. "When I reflect on where my life is when we started out with nothing—a lot of it is hard work and smarts, but a lot is having somebody help you out in life." He wanted to be that person for Porscha.

Porscha quickly stood out among the Cody students in MAP and wanted to land one of the coveted summer Launch internships at Ernst & Young at the end of her first year at Michigan State. To do so, she would be competing against other minority candidates from much healthier and wealthier backgrounds and schools. Ernst & Young sponsors the Launch internship to build a more diverse workforce. For young people of color, the Launch internship can lead to a long and lucrative career at Ernst & Young. George was eager to see Porscha win an internship, but he removed himself from the interview process, not wanting to have any undue influence over it. He was confident she would shine on her own.

The morning of the interview, Porscha was a no-show. Ernst & Young hosts a reception for the candidates the night before the interviews and pays for them all to spend the night in the luxurious Book Cadillac Hotel. But she chose to skip out on that.

"I had family issues," Porscha recalls. "I wanted to stay home that night to be with my mom and sister, and my mom took the car to work the next morning. So I needed to get a ride with my grandad, and he's real slow." When Porscha finally made it to the interview, she was thirty minutes late.

"She was also completely unprepared, with a beret and outfit that showed she didn't know about the firm," George said. "Our interview team didn't want to let her in, and they called me, and I told them okay, this is a great life lesson for her. What made her special was her work ethic. I didn't want her to go through life thinking people would be handing her things."

"I had to go down to the lobby and have a real tough talk about dress code and the people in her life I didn't think were good for her. That's a real tough thing to say and tougher to hear. But I talked to her like a father. I also talked to her about my disappointment, because I was disappointed. I had invested a lot. And I had offered to coach her, but she never took me up on it."

This was one of those times in life that can be a defining moment or a breaking point. Porscha chose to let it be a defining one.

"George always wants me to get to a better place so I can help my family and not end up in the same place we are already in, but that's easier said than done," Porscha observes. "I follow his advice sometimes, but not all the time."

"Fast forward a year," George says. "Porscha is back on the interview list, and to her credit, she took the time to call me, talked to other Ernst & Young people, went to the Ernst & Young multicultural business center, came to the event the night before. She not only got the internship, she was ranked number one from a lot of people who didn't know her and couldn't figure out why they didn't hire her last year."

Over the course of their friendship, George was named CEO of Ernst & Young in Michigan. Despite the demands on his time, he drives up to East Lansing two or three times a year to see Porscha at college and has lunch with her when she comes home on break.

"She doesn't really ask me for anything," George says.

You think these kids are going to be asking you for money. She doesn't. She wants your time. She wants a text every once in a while. She wants to hear your voice. There's a commitment up front because you gotta get a bond, but when you get beyond that, it's kind of like, "Once my daughter makes it to college, what does my daughter need from me?" It's really, "Hey, I'm transitioning into an adult. I need some guidance. I need some coaching."

Porscha's become an extension of my family. I didn't come from a wealthy background. My parents didn't go to college. I was lucky enough to have some people who steered me in the right direction. Part of it is lucky. Part of it is having somebody who reaches out to you and says "You know what, you are better than you think you are." And it's up to you with what you do with that challenge.[2]

Even when she doesn't take his advice, Porscha still finds strength in her relationship with George. "If I fail, he is there to uplift me. If I have doubts, he encourages me," she says. "He makes me feel like he's always there for me with a positive look at negative times."

Ernst & Young's College MAP program started in 2008 and has reached almost one thousand young people in purposeful friendships like the one George and Porscha share. Other companies would be smart to follow.

RADICAL ENGAGEMENT

The most sought-after talent today—the millennials coming out of the best business schools and universities in the country—want to know that the company they are working for is making a difference. They want to be a part of something bigger than themselves, and the traditional form of corporate outreach is not cutting it for their companies anymore. They too have done the career days, the job fairs, and the school-supply drives. They have read to kindergarten classes as a part of National Reading Month and have painted school hallways as part of Martin Luther King Day activities. They are not making the difference they crave within traditional corporate structures.

The zeitgeist of the millennials is as important to the survival of the church as it is to corporate America. Billy Thrall, who leads the Arizona Governor's Office of Faith-Based Initiatives, sees this throughout his state. He says, "As churches get younger—and if they are going to survive they have to get younger—for that generation this has to be holistic Christianity. They are hit on their cell phone with world news. They are saying, 'How does Jesus matter to the world around me?'"

McKinsey and Company offers a helpful perspective in its analysis of the challenge before corporate America. "Traditional corporate social responsibility (CSR) is failing to deliver, for both companies and society." Most companies pursue unrelated strategies at the whim of their executives. The result is "a hodgepodge of uncoordinated CSR and philanthropic activities disconnected from the company's strategy that neither make any meaningful social impact nor strengthen the firm's long-term competitiveness." McKinsey's recommendation? They suggest that a company should carve out a specific cause or outcome that it can dedicate itself to, get to know the stakeholders in that area well, apply best management practices to the solution and to "engage radically."[3]

This is exactly what Mark Reuss did as the president of GM North America when he teamed up with the United Way in Detroit to double the number of schools in United Way's turnaround movement. Because of his commitment, and the backing of the GM Foundation, the United Way in Detroit was able to invite the remaining failing high schools of the city to join them in a community-wide turnaround effort. Seven schools formed the GM Network of Excellence. Along with the eight schools from the first network, fifteen schools across Metro Detroit were committed to graduating more than 80 percent of their kids where retention rates of less than 60 percent had existed for years before.

Mark is known affectionately around GM as "a car guy," which is high praise in the Motor City. Tall, broad shouldered, with a mischievous smile that belies the lines chiseled deep into his face, he looks like a high school football coach who had once been a wild linebacker back in the day. His is the type of person who would commit to taking on the city's toughest high schools while also helping to run GM. And despite making the biggest investment in the GM Foundation's history, Mark was always clear that the success of the schools would not happen with money alone. He knew from his own dad how much it meant to be personally involved in making a change.

"My parents came from a small farming town in southern Illinois, from humble beginnings. My mom was seventeen when they got married. All they had when they moved up here was a car and the money they got from their wedding."[4]

Mark's father, Lloyd Reuss, pumped gas at night back in 1957 while he started out as an engineer-in-training at GM. He rose through the ranks to become president of GM in 1990. Many thought Lloyd would become GM's next CEO, but he was unexpectedly fired two years later in a sweeping top-management change initiated by GM's board of directors to shake up the culture at the company. Mark was twenty-nine and a mid-level engineer for GM when his mother called to tell him the news.[5] Less than twenty years later, Mark had risen to a position similar to his dad as the President of GM North America. In this position he decided to make a major investment in turning around Detroit's most troubled high schools.

"When my dad was let go from GM, he was not old. A lot of his colleagues who were also let go left and went to their homes in Naples and all that stuff. He didn't. He's still in the same house I grew up in. What he did was help Father Cunningham and

Eleanor Josaitis run Focus: HOPE. It consumed him. That's what he helped grow for the last twenty years. That's what he does every day. That's a huge model. I was around that my whole life. I still am."

Focus: HOPE is a Detroit institution founded to foster racial healing after the notorious Detroit riots in 1967. In helping its founders grow the organization to increase job training opportunities for thousands of Detroiters, Lloyd Reuss was taking on one of the most difficult societal challenges of the last generation. His son is now doing the same for the most difficult social challenge of this generation.

For Mark, stewarding GM out of bankruptcy meant more than making great cars and great profits again, it meant "doing something dramatic" for Detroit, and he wanted GM's people front and center in the work. But for a company coming out of bankruptcy in a very difficult industry, it proved difficult to get his employees to also find the time to give to students at one of the seven high schools in GM's new Network of Excellence schools. Reuss tapped seven of his rising stars to become a champion for each school. They served on a council of volunteer champions who met monthly with school leaders and students to help them define and achieve their annual goals. GM also sent teams of people to conduct mock interviews with students at their schools, and hundreds of students came to GM each year to do job shadows with GM employees. But the relationships were still too distant and infrequent, the impact still too small, for Reuss.

"I was sitting in this office and talking with Mary Barra and William Jones from Focus: HOPE," Mark recalls. They talked about the schools in the GM Network and what happens to those students during the summer, and they created the idea of a "GM Student Corps"—an opportunity for ten students in each of their schools to be employed by GM, making a difference in their community during the summer. Mark said,

Our relationship with our retirees prior to bankruptcy was horrible. There's so many good people that are retired from here. So many. And the parenting piece for children is variable. What if we linked them with a real role model that actually had success in business? And what if we created the opportunity for those relationships to happen? And show them what it means to show up. To have money in your pocket. To be there.

From that conversation, GM Student Corps was born, creating new pathways for retirees to build meaningful relationships with young people battling to get out of poverty. GM Student Corps is an idea much like Ernst & Young's College MAP in that it intentionally creates easy on-ramps for people to build purposeful relationships with young people to help them overcome the challenges of poverty.

Mark's first phone call went to Mike DiGiovanni, an economist and well-respected GM executive who had run Hummer and GMC before retiring to teach at a local university. In Mike, Mark knew that he had a well-connected insider who knew how to get things done. What he did not know is that Mike was actually quite like many of the students they meant to serve.

Mike grew up on the west side of Detroit. His dad had worked in produce and would go down to the Eastern Market at 4 a.m. to get the best deals from the farmers, and he wouldn't get home until 8 each night, after his shop had closed. The long hours and stress of work took their toll. When Mike was in ninth grade at University of Detroit Jesuit High School, his father died suddenly of a heart attack. Mike's two older brothers were already out of the house, leaving Mike alone with his devastated mother. With no real work history, his mother cleaned houses to help them get by. But they could no longer afford U of D High. They couldn't even afford their house. Mike and his mother were put out of their own home, and depended on the generosity of his aunt for shelter.

Mike recalls, "My mom couldn't drive, so she would walk to the grocery store and get all the wilted vegetables before they threw them away. To the day she died, she rolled a cart to the grocery store looking for deals. I would have to go over to her house and throw food out, telling her, 'you cannot eat this stuff!'" He pauses, reflecting, stuffing back the emotion in his throat and concludes, "She was an amazing lady."[6]

Even though he lost his home and had no real income, Mike was able to stay at U of D High, an all-boys, private high school, for the next three years because of a Jonathan in his life, Father Patrick Rice, a Jesuit priest who was also the ninth-grade counselor at that time. He took an interest in Mike and made sure the Jesuits did everything they could to help Mike make it through high school. After graduation, Mike went on to get a full scholarship to the University of Detroit for college and then received a graduate teaching fellowship that paid for his master's degree in economics. Mike didn't have to pay for three years of private high school or either of his degrees because a compassionate counselor saw a scared kid virtually alone in the world and made a covenant with him that he would see him through to graduation.

After sending GM so many resumés that they actually wrote him a letter asking him not to apply for any more jobs, Mike kept applying and finally landed a job well below the one he held at the US Army Corps of Engineers. But Mike wanted to work at GM since he was a five-year-old kid who could name every car on the road. He took the job and reached the top tiers of leadership over the next thirty years, including running the Hummer division in its heyday. He now runs GM Student Corps, aimed at students just like him.

"When Mark called me to talk about Student Corps," Mike remembers,

> he told me he wanted to do something for the kids who were in the schools and weren't going to be able to make it to college. He wanted to get them a good job on their resumé and to teach them a skill. But as it turns out, they all want to go to college. It turns out, these kids are just like plants that need water. When our retirees got involved, it was unlike anything we ever expected. They bloomed. Man, they just bloomed more than we could have imagined!

Brittany Agee is one of those people who bloomed. She describes herself as a three on Matthews's scale when she came to Cody. She was a shy, angry kid who was more disposed to shutting down than to showing up. No one in Brittany's family had ever graduated from high school. Her father died when she was nine. Her mother was not a stable presence in her life, so she lived with her grandmother. That in itself is a lot for a kids to handle, but then her grandmother was killed by a stray bullet from a neighbor fighting off a carjacker.[7] By the age of thirteen, she had lost her home and the three people in her life who had given her one. If not for her Aunt Cassandra, who stepped in to give her a home despite her own challenge of being blind, Brittany would have likely become a ward of the state.

Johnathon Matthews and the teachers at APL kept after Brittany, never failing in their belief that she could rise to be a one on Matthews's scale. They encouraged her to apply for GM's new

Student Corps, which she did. She had no idea what she was getting into.

AWESOME AIN'T EASY

Dawin Wright is the no-nonsense leader of GM's Student Corps at Cody. Every Student Corps member will tell you Dawin's mantra, "Awesome ain't easy." He says it a lot in a culture where mediocrity has become excellence, and less than mediocre has become normal. He learned the value of family and hard work growing up with three brothers as the son of a sharecropper in Arkansas. When he was a child, his family became part of "the great migration" of southern blacks who moved north to escape the Jim Crow South. His dad and all eight of his dad's siblings moved to the same neighborhood on the west side of Chicago and attended the same church together. Dawin graduated from Farragut High School in the late 1960s, a school that reminds him of the old Cody. Six hundred young people started out with him as freshmen, and only three hundred of them graduated four years later.

After college, Dawin went from teaching auto technology at a community college to a job with GM helping to improve its relationships with some of its most challenging dealerships in Chicago. His success there launched a unique rise for an African American at GM in the 1970s. At thirty-seven, he was promoted to the executive ranks, just twelve years from his start with the company.

As a new executive, Dawin sought out a mentorship with Barbara Mahone, the highest ranking African American female executive in GM's history at that time. "She had no idea who I was, but she did it anyway. Barbara taught me what it means to be true to yourself and to lose yourself to something bigger and greater than you. She developed more African Americans into leaders than anyone else I know at GM. It's twenty-seven years later, and we still have lunch together six or seven times a year."[8]

Cody's Student Corps members respond well to Dawin's challenge to be awesome, but it does take time. "When Brittany first came into Student Corps, I could see that she was a sensitive young lady masquerading behind a wall of indifference and 'I don't care,'" Dawin recalls. "She was afraid to give because she thought all of life was take. She held large pity parties as a pure defense mechanism, and the personal side of her life was all collateral damage."

The negative stuff in Brittany's life was choking the life out of her, but Dawin helped her to see that we learn more from the negative things in life than the positive ones, and that the negative things she had overcome were helping her to be stronger than most other people. Brittany went from being a person who showed no emotion to one who was giving advice to others to being the first in her family to go to college when no one else had made it through high school. Dawin is quick to point out that it takes time for young people to break through. "Brittany was that far into it, into being 'hard' in order to survive," he says.

A turning point for Brittany occurred on February 9, 2013. It was the day after her sixteenth birthday, and Brittany was meeting with Dawin, Tom, and Marilyn, the three GM retirees of Cody's Student Corps, to go over her first-semester report card with them, a meeting they hold with their students every quarter. A few minutes into their discussion about her progress, Brittany's hard exterior turned into tears she fought to hold back.

"No one cares about what grades I got or what my GPA is," Brittany said. She had earned a 4.0 GPA for the first time and wanted to share it with her mother, but her mother wasn't there.

"I found out yesterday what I'm worth," she said. "And I'm not worth two dollars. Two dollars! And I'm not worth that." Tears flooded her eyes and the eyes of others in the room. Two dollars is what it would have cost for her mother to take the bus across town to wish Brittany a happy birthday on her Sweet Sixteen the day before, but she couldn't manage that. It crushed Brittany's spirit. Dawin was sitting across the table questioning her about her grades. He was the only one who could respond.

"I would not hug the young ladies in Student Corps," Dawin says. "So many of them have been so mistreated by men that it would not be appropriate. When girls broke down in sessions I was leading, I'd always ask Marilyn to give them a hug, as I would do for the young men. But I hugged Brittany and told her that dollars don't define her and that people don't define her, that there was so much more to her than that." A father's love in that moment restored Brittany's soul.

Dawin is doing for young people at Cody what Barbara Mahone did for him and others like him at GM, but he is not the only one enjoying the adventure. GM has sixty retirees doing the same each summer. They range from former brand managers to former plant managers and all positions in between. One of them, Debbie Easternhall, even drives three hours from Ohio to Detroit each day because she enjoys it so much.

It took Cody a couple years to get to the point that it would be ready for a group of outsiders to come in to the school. Even then, when Student Corps was first launched, the principals had to convince students to give it a try. Now, it's a coveted position in a highly competitive process. When those retirees kept showing up every day during an incredibly hot summer, they built trust with the kids in Student Corps. When GM and the retirees came back the next summer, and the summer after that, they built trust with the school and a whole bunch of young people who weren't in Student Corps but saw the difference it was making in the lives of their friends. It started to become expected for young people to try new experiences offered at the school. It paved the way for Oak Pointe to launch.

What Cody did with Oak Pointe Church expanded that paradigm even wider. One of the biggest challenges facing the school is how unprepared its freshmen are—not just academically, but mentally and emotionally. Matthews and Kurt Alber from Oak Pointe Church came up with the idea of having their Oak Pointe's members mentor the twelfth graders to help them mentor the ninth graders in order to speed up their development. Sounds like a great idea in theory, but in practice it meant twenty mostly older, white, affluent suburban people connecting with young people nothing like them demographically. The idea would have been preposterous a few years ago. It still sounded pretty far-fetched to the seniors now, but they trusted Matthews, at least enough to give it a try.

Brittany Agee captures that sentiment well: "When we came to the meeting with a whole bunch of different looking people, I was like, *Why should I talk to these people? They don't look nothing like me.*"[9]

The students did a series of round-robin interviews, almost like speed dating, and Brittany quickly connected with Melissa Meadows, a single mother of three working two jobs who had been through her own trauma during a difficult divorce. Melissa had a lot going on in her own life, certainly enough to say no to the idea of driving down to Cody during lunch every other week to meet with students. But she felt God calling her to this when her pastor, Bob Shirock, spoke about it at church week after week. She has learned to follow that calling.

I had no time, no money, and a lot of stress already in my life. But I just showed up at Cody and asked Brittany what she wanted. She said that she wanted consistency—someone who would keep showing up. I decided to do that and to trust God to make it work because I wanted to show my kids to trust God.

Melissa and Brittany didn't just see each other every other Monday. They hung out on weekends. Sometimes Melissa picked Brittany up to go to church with them. Other times, she'd take her out to a cultural event in the city or have her over for dinner. These things matter a lot to Brittany.

I told Matthews I had never sat down at a table and had dinner like a normal family. When we cook in our house, we all go our separate ways. I'll watch a movie or something. I was like, "Dang, I had never really sat down for dinner as a family."

I was telling Melissa this, but I didn't think she was going to do it with me. And she was like, "Well, you can come over to my house. I can cook dinner one day." And I thought she was just saying that. But one day we actually did do it, and it's real different from what I'm used to. She actually took me to her house. Most people wouldn't do that. We sat down at her house and were just talking and stuff. And I'm thinking to myself, *Wow, we are really sitting down eating dinner as a family. It's crazy.* She does a lot of stuff most people wouldn't do.

When Brittany joins Melissa for church at Oak Pointe, it's twenty miles and a world away from Brittany's home. That doesn't keep Brittany from offering them some advice.

Their church—whooh! It's way different than churches in the neighborhood. In some churches, they may not take a person who comes in with a lot of tattoos and piercings or something. One of their pastors had a whole bunch of tattoos. I was like, "At the next church, they're going to look at you like you're crazy. They will make you cover them up." But they take you as you are.

Brittany is heading off to school in a few days at Alabama State University. Melissa will drive Brittany, her aunt, and her good friend and high school classmate Aiesha, the eight hundred miles to school, and then drive home with Brittany's aunt. "God showed up in amazing ways," Melissa says. "He provided for me financially in ways that we could help provide for Brittany. And I think it showed Brittany what is possible when you have God in your life."

All the logic in the world would have told Melissa that she did not have enough time in her life to drive to Cody for lunch every two weeks. Who was she to think she could make a difference? But God knew what he was doing: Brittany's resilience has been a salve to the wounds of divorce that Melissa's children felt, and Melissa and her kids are closer and stronger because of their time together with Brittany. "We need Brittany as much as Brittany needs us," Melissa says.

The same holds true for Brittany:

I was talking to my sister, and she was like, "How do you keep getting all these good people in your life?" I looked at her like, "God has blessed me with all these people because I don't have parents." My sister has a mom and a stepdad. I don't have that stable household like she has. I don't know what I'd do without Auntie Cassandra and Melissa and Dawin and

Matthews. Those people who showed me they care. Because my life could have gone way different than the way it did.

A relationship between Jonathan and David gives as much to Jonathan as it does to David, but Jonathan has to be willing to step in. When he does, it creates a foundation for things to follow that he could never have planned or expected. George Lenyo mentored one person through a College MAP program that only reached ten students the first year. GM Student Corps only hires 130 students each summer at ten different schools. Oak Pointe Church started with twenty students this past school year. But the impact of these small groups of people is reaching far beyond the students they touch. It is changing the culture of the school and the perspectives and experiences of the students in it, as those students contagiously influence the lives of their friends and classmates. This is the effect that you and your church can have when you answer the call to be a friend like Jonathan was to David.

You don't have to have the whole thing scripted and figured out to do this. God already has that figured out for you. All you have to do is seek him and have an ear to hear his will and the heart to do what he tells you. When you do that, you will find time and ideas you did not have before. And you will do all types of things. Send your David a text. Take them out for lunch. Call them on your way home from work. Get their mother something special for Christmas. Pay for their driver's ed. Tell them about the challenges you are having at work or at home. Have a birthday party for them at your house. Help them set goals and together think through the obstacles to those goals. So many huge obstacles to a child in poverty can be fairly easily overcome by a friend with some connections and a little bit of extra income to share. Stop by the school unexpectedly and give your David a ride home. Take them back-to-school shopping for clothes and supplies—and be sure to buy some socks, underwear and T-shirts. Tell them the hard truths in love about things they are doing wrong—whether it's the friends they're choosing or not saying please and thank you when ordering a meal.

When you decide to be Jonathan to a young person in need, God will fill your heart with opportunities and ideas to remind them of their identity in the Lord and to help them achieve their destiny. It takes churches and companies to provide the pathway for this, and then it takes people willing to honor that still, small voice that tells us to step out of our comfort zone. When we do, we will be strengthened by the challenges and triumphs of helping young people win their battle against poverty.

Making Money

Almost a year to the day after Keyvon graduated from high school, I was able to put my law degree to use and successfully defended him on the charge of Entering Without Permission. Okay, maybe that's a little bit of a stretch. We actually won the case because the cop didn't show up. Still, a win is a win, and I felt like Matlock. Only after it was over did I learn how worried Keyvon was that he was going to be sent back to jail. We enjoyed a good ride away from the court house that day.

A couple of months after that, Keyvon and I planned to meet for lunch. He told me to meet him at the corner of Fenkell and Trinity in the Brightmoor neighborhood in northwest Detroit. This stretch of Fenkell has motorcycle clubs that are active at night, and prostitutes that are active in the middle of the day. I figured he was staying in another abandoned house and didn't want me to see how bad he was living.

When I got to the corner, he was nowhere to be seen. I turned my head around to the right to see if he was behind me, and he appeared out of nowhere on my left. We drove over to Telegraph, hoping to find a decent Coney Island but had to settle for McDonald's. When we finished ordering our food, Keyvon reached into his pocket to try to pay, something he hadn't been able to do in a long, long time. It caught me off-guard.

Keyvon had added mass back to his muscular frame. Wearing a black T-shirt and jeans, he could have passed for a soldier coming out of boot camp in the best shape of his life. He had broken up with his girlfriend, the mother of Keyvon Jr. Actually she left him for some other guy. He had bought her and Junior new outfits for Mother's Day, but she never came to see him—that day or for weeks after that. He returned her outfit, and "shed some tears that day." But he was seeing another girl now, and still taking care of Junior as best he could. He and his son's mother had been a great couple together, better to each other than many married couples I count as friends. This was a huge loss for him.

The cops had found his Lincoln, but it had been broken down ever since. He paid his brother's dad $500 to put a new engine in it, but it needed about $1,000 more in repairs. Keyvon had the money saved up and stored away safely at his mother's place, but his brother's dad hadn't gotten around to finishing the job. For every step forward there was a "but."

Over our Quarter Pounders and fries, Keyvon confided in me that he had started selling drugs, and not just small bags of weed, to folks in the neighborhood to make a few bucks. He was selling heroin to a customer base made up mostly of working-class white men who drove in from the suburbs to the spot I picked him up for lunch.

I felt like I was supposed to yell at him about what a dangerous thing he was doing. I could have threatened to stop our relationship until he stopped. Perhaps I should have. But I was so relieved to see him healthy and eating regularly, and I felt like this was an even more important time for us to remain friends so I could help him find an alternative job. We talked through the risks and benefits of his work, and he explained convincingly how he had minimized his risks of getting arrested or shot. At this point in our friendship, I cared less about the impact of his employment on his customers than I did about him. I was relieved to see him a bit further from the edge of hunger and desperation, despite how much closer it pushed him to the prospect of prison.

Still, winter was only a few months away, and he had no home of his own. Hoping to encourage him to take a safer job, I told him that Maritza and I would pay for the first month's rent of an apartment for him—as long as he got a legal job with a real paycheck. I wasn't sure what would happen next. Then Keyvon stopped returning my calls.

7

What to Watch Out For

On July 2, 2009, twenty students were waiting at a bus stop outside of a gas station on Warren Road in Detroit. Most of them had just finished taking summer school classes to get the credits they missed by failing classes at Cody High the previous school year. One of them had been in a fight earlier in the day, and he was eager to get home to safety. The others were just glad to be out of school and ready to enjoy a good summer evening in the city.

That all changed when two boys ran out of the gas station with guns drawn and T-shirts pulled over their faces to conceal their identity. Before anyone had a chance to react, the boys began firing at them, hoping to hit the boy they had fought with earlier that day. When the shooting stopped, seven students lay on the ground with at least one bullet in them, writhing in pain while blood flowed out of their bodies.

Johnathon Matthews was at a training in Connecticut at the time. He had spent a year working with his teachers on plans to transform Cody High School into four smaller schools in the same building. He caught the first plane to Detroit when he heard the news and went to the hospital to check in on his students. What he discovered changed the way he thought about school.

"Many of the victims were former Cody students, students that we had just kicked out and left for gone. And that's when I realized that, just as police can't arrest their way out of crime, we can't kick students out and think that all of a sudden things will get better. Those young people still exist."[1]

Miraculously, all seven of the children survived. The experience foreshadowed the challenges that lay ahead and God's grace in the midst of them. It cemented in Matthews a determination to stop suspending and expelling students as the solution for his most difficult students.

COUNT THE COSTS

Jesus warned his followers that they better be prepared to carry their cross if they want to be his disciples. "Suppose one of you wants to build a tower," he says in Luke. "Won't you first sit down and estimate the cost to see if you have enough money to complete it? For if you lay the foundation and are not able to finish it, everyone who sees it will ridicule you, saying, 'This person began to build and wasn't able to finish'" (Lk 14:28-30).

The worst thing your church or company can do is start a partnership with a school and not see it through. If you make a commitment to help a troubled school, troubles will arise. It's important for you to count the costs before you make a commitment to them. When the troubles come, will you retreat? Or will you learn from the experience, as Matthews did, to strengthen your resolve and your plans to succeed? The world around the school, and life inside of it, can be hurtful.

When you commit to partner with a school or to become a Jonathan to a young person, you will likely enter into a relationship not just with that person but with the adults in their world: their teachers, family members, and other school staff and partners. This tapestry of relationships will give texture to your life, but unknowingly you may be running into a minefield filled with negative experiences, unconscious assumptions, and deeply held beliefs about the way the world works, the school should be run, and children should be raised. Differences in culture, race, religion, and income cause unintended pain, more so with the adult who has been hurt and hardened than the young person. The purpose of this chapter is to help you avoid setting off those triggers, and to encourage you to engage in the power of seeking and giving forgiveness freely when you do hurt others or are hurt by them.

RELIGION DOS AND DON'TS

Lead with love. Schools have such a long history of striving to keep religion out that they may forget that they cannot discriminate against a person or group on the basis of their religion. You should overcommunicate that you and your church intend to love the students right where they are, and that you want to partner with the school to determine how to best serve its needs. This means your people will serve concessions at games, help coach robotics teams or the debate club, or help make meals for teachers during parent-teacher conferences, as long as these needs are giving your people consistent opportunities to build relationships with students.

You should also state repeatedly that you are not here to proselytize. This word gets to the heart of most people's fears that you will come in and force your beliefs on them or their students. You shouldn't do this, and you should be upfront about the fact that you won't.

Finally, you should be clear that you will be honest about who you are if anybody asks. Your religion will come up in conversations as you build relationships, and neither the Constitution nor the Supreme Court requires you to lie about who you are.

Once you are in the school, you do not have a constitutional right to organize a religious club or organize group prayers. Those things can be organized and led by students within a school and are afforded constitutional protection, but adult-led activities like this are not. You are, however, free to invite people you are in relationship with to your church or to ask them if they would like you to pray for them, or to share your story with them. But lead with love. If you wantonly walk around the school posting flyers about your church service or telling your story loosely, you are making it more about your church and you than the school and its students. On the other hand, if you serve meals to a sports team before home games or work with student leaders on a community service project, and you invite them to church and breakfast afterwards, the trust you have built with them makes the invitation a natural part of your relationship, not an awkward attempt at proselytization.

PROFESSIONALS VERSUS VOLUNTEERS

One of the biggest challenges to this work may be that many school leaders and teachers don't "get" volunteers. Most educators have been trained to succeed in a control-and-command environment. The principal controls the teachers. The teachers control their students. They are both focused on making it through to the end of the day so they can go home and check papers or prepare lesson plans for the next day. They are not thinking about how to get more people to come into the school; that only adds more variables to an already overextended day. Educators uniformly want more parental involvement and more services to support their students, but they have very little time or money to make either happen. Turning some of these things over to volunteers they don't know can be more difficult than accepting the status quo.

Therefore, schools with huge needs for caring volunteers may not seem receptive to them. An offshoot of a command-and-control environment is that it becomes easier to acquiesce than to engage. News about your partnership in a staff meeting may lead to a lot of people nodding and smiling affirmatively, while thinking to themselves, *This will never happen.* They've seen a lot of people, partnerships, and programs come and go.

This is why it's important to look for ways your church can make a meaningful difference for a school early in the courtship phase, and also to secure a commitment that your liaison will be a regular member of their leadership team meetings. You must give school staff a working reference point for what love in action looks like. It's also why it's so important to establish a beachhead in the school once the partnership begins. People other than the leader must have a chance to see and feel the love that you are bringing in consistent and unexpected ways.

COMMUNICATION WITH PRINCIPALS

Don't assume that the world inside the school works the way yours does, and don't assume that your way is better. Most principals I know rarely return phone calls or emails from strangers. People accustomed to doing business this way often interpret a principal's failure to respond in a timely fashion as a lack of interest or professionalism. A promising partnership can wither in its infancy because of this misunderstanding. What we fail to understand is that principals spend most of their days responding to the people and issues directly in front of them.

Emails and meeting requests from strangers are on the bottom of their list of pressing needs.

The best way to get in contact with a principal you don't know is to go to the school, be especially courteous and genuine to the people at the front desk, and ask to see the principal for just a few minutes. Then, be prepared to wait for a little bit and to walk around with the principal when the time comes. You will likely get more than a few minutes with them because they will enjoy the variety and opportunity that you bring. Just be sure to ask for the principal's cell number before you leave. Most principals who ignore emails respond to texts with lightning speed. While I have never been able to get a meeting with the CEO of a business this way, it works with great frequency with school leaders. But I have heard many people complain about principals' failures to respond to their emails instead of understanding and embracing what works best for their world.

CULTURE AND CLIMATE

Once inside the school, it may be shocking to hear the amount of cussing in hallway conversations or to see the yelling, smacking, and horseplay that verges on violence. This won't be evident at first. The most dangerous schools have an uncanny ability to create the appearance of safety and order when a group of visitors is in the building. Their staff takes great pride in their ability to lock down the campus on special days, and even the students are willing conspirators in keeping the hallways respectful and orderly. The first few times you come to a school, you will likely find things to be running smoothly.

When you create a consistent presence at the school, you will begin to see it function as it normally does, and here's the challenge: many things that should be unacceptable have, over time, become normal. You may see large numbers of students coming to school late, some without jackets in the winter, some smelling of marijuana, and some getting handled roughly by security guards as they make their way through the metal detectors. You may see teachers in classrooms who have lost control of their class or their tempers. You may see roofs leaking, ceiling tiles falling, computer labs without working computers, and classrooms still waiting for a teacher two months into the school year. None of this should be normal. If you raise every issue you see, you will likely come off as naive or insensitive to the challenges of the school and community. If you don't say or do anything, why are you there? How do you respond?

Walk in prayer. An influx of new people in a school can positively impact the culture of the school. What has become normal need not be that way. But that change takes time and comes through shared experiences in trusted friendships and counsel—not through driveby advice and a spirit of superiority from school visitors. The principal and teachers see the same things you see, but they have not had enough time, support, and collective will power to change everything they would like. Even when they do, change does not come overnight.

The best advice for managing this tension comes from Young Life, a Christian ministry in 4,200 schools nationwide. They believe that adults coming into a school have to earn the right to be heard, and this does not occur until the adult knows by name seventy-five students in the school. That may seem unreasonable. Shouldn't kids just respect adults? Can I remember that many kids' names? Unreasonable or not, it is the most practical advice you or your church can follow for building an abiding presence in the school. If you keep in mind that you don't have the right to comment on or try to fix a problem as big as school culture until you know seventy-five students by name, you will likely have a much more thoughtful perspective, one which will likely be received much better as well.

THE SAVIOR COMPLEX

If you are not careful, you or other members of your church or company can unknowingly exude a know-it-all attitude. A great primer for those thinking about getting involved in this type of ministry is *When Helping Hurts: How to Alleviate Poverty Without Hurting the Poor and Yourself* by Steve Corbett and Brian Fikkert. They explain the dangers of the economically well-off assuming a god-complex, which they define as "a subtle and unconscious sense of superiority in which they believe that they have achieved their wealth through their own efforts and that they have been anointed to decide what is best for low-income people, whom they view as inferior to themselves."[2] This is *the* problem to be avoided. The authors observe,

> The way that we act toward the economically poor often communicates—albeit unintentionally—that we are superior and they are inferior. In the process we hurt the poor and ourselves. And here is the clincher: this dynamic is likely to be particularly strong whenever middle- to upper-class, North American Christians try to help the poor, given these Christians' tendency toward a Western, materialistic perspective of the nature of poverty.[3]

This is why it is particularly important to be a friend, not a mentor, to work with, not to do for, and to remember that we are all broken and in need of the Savior, not to think of ourselves as a savior.

The authors' solution? "Avoid Paternalism. Do not do things for people that they can do for themselves." That includes "knowledge paternalism" (I have all the answers) and "management paternalism" (I can take charge of this and make it hum in no time) as well as "labor paternalism" (We can get this school cleaned up while the kids are on break).[4]

That doesn't mean you should simply accept everything as it is either. Scripture does require us to act justly, but to do it with mercy as we walk humbly with God (Mic 6:8). Your presence and perspective can give strength to others.

When Oak Pointe began its partnership with Cody, cussing in the hallways had become commonplace. It wasn't unusual for a student to cuss out a teacher in the classroom, or even to hear a staff member cussing in front of the students—especially the security guards, who were only a few years older than the students, or the coaches, who were often from and still living in the same neighborhoods as the students. Kurt Alber, Oak Pointe's liaison, raised the question with the principals of when it is acceptable for adults to cuss. Which adults? Why? He also worked with staff and students in retreats on helping each school to determine the core values it lived by.

In the second year of the partnership, the students and staff at Cody began a joint effort to "reverse the curse." They agreed to make the school a cuss-free campus despite its being a longtime norm. This would have been inconceivable in the first few years of the schools' turnaround. But over eight years the campus moved from being violent to being safe, then from being safe to being serious about getting kids into college, then from getting kids into college to actually finishing and succeeding in the world. In this latter context, staff and students alike saw the wanton cussing as inconsistent with what they want out of life— but it took eight years to get there. The movement has a stronger likelihood to last because it is coming from inside the school instead of being imposed from the outside. And it's also helpful to note that it was outside partners who repeatedly raised the issue with school leadership, and then helped to facilitate the meetings that led to the campaign. By consistently raising the question in discreet ways, and helping the school bring together a group of people who could do something about it, they put the school in a position to own a better environment for itself.

RACE ISSUES

The school partnerships that form the foundation for the Jonathan Effect started years ago with Tony Evans's African American church and the predominately African American churches that followed. In addition, many African Americans already working in the schools as teachers, coaches, counselors, principals, and community partners make and keep Jonathan Commitments to young people all the time. While African American churches and Christians can do more, plenty are already doing a lot. I am writing to encourage them to do more, and I am writing to inspire other churches to do so as well.

A predominately white church can partner with a predominately African American or Latino school. I've heard it said that young people need mirrors and windows. They need to have mirrors—meaningful relationships with people from their neighborhood or people who look like them—but they also need windows—people who have a different vista or background who may show them other perspectives.

If you are a white person going into a school where you are the minority, you may want to keep a few things in mind.

1. Act like you've been there before. When Barry Sanders scored a touchdown, he handed the ball to the ref and acted like it

was no big deal. This is not time to walk into rooms or relationships with wide eyes making comments about how different things are. Don't act cool, but do your best to be cool.

2. Never call attention to the color of your skin or other differences, especially with young people. When you are in a group setting or even talking one-on-one, there is no need to make jokes about or refer to the fact that you are a different color or from a different background. Young people already see that, and they don't have nearly as many negative experiences about it as do people over the age of forty. Referring to your color will make things awkward. At a point when they are trying to make a connection to you, don't tell them that you are different. Help them find a bond instead.

3. Make a connection—any connection. Say something or do something of value to the conversation. In my experience, people of color pay much more attention to the actions of whites in a room than white people pay to their own actions or inaction. When you are often in the minority, you have to be on the lookout for what others are thinking or may be thinking about you. White people unaccustomed to being in the minority haven't had these senses sharpened, and I have seen them walk into and out of a good meeting seemingly unaware of how their silence or their body language conveyed a message other than the one they meant. They may have been challenged and inspired, but they didn't want to speak up or be noticed because of their discomfort at being in the minority, and they didn't realize that their silence looked like they didn't care or want to be there. A simple way to avoid this is to smile. If you are naturally shy, nod or shake your head affirmatively while someone else is talking. Talk

one-on-one with somebody before the meeting starts or after it ends. Help to serve food or clean up afterwards. Say or do something to make a connection with somebody. If you don't, you will likely be perceived as just another white person who doesn't care, regardless of how you actually feel.

As you build trusting relationships with people who don't look like you, especially those over thirty, you may begin to find yourself in conversations where race comes up. At times, it can come up in offensive or confrontational ways, especially as others come to like and trust you. You may find yourself hearing a passionate argument that the government brought crack cocaine into America to keep black people down or that white people are trying to destroy public schools because they don't care about black people. You may hear that white people don't make good parents because they don't discipline their children or that the criminal justice system is being used to keep black people in slavery. You may feel your face turning red, your heart jumping into your mouth, and maybe that somebody in the room called you a racist. You can respond the way most people would and argue back from your own experience and emotions. Take it from me: this never works. Healing and much deeper friendships follow when white people do a few things more often:

1. Listen! African Americans rarely get a chance to talk to white people about things that cause them pain without being told that they are wrong or having to tiptoe around the white person's feelings. Just being a good listener and not forcing your opinion on the speaker can be a unique gift of its own to you and to the person you are talking with.

2. Ask if it's okay to offer a different perspective. In most of my life and relationships, I am a minority white person in a

room. I feel very comfortable having race conversations. But when difficult issues of race come up, I have learned to ask for permission to say something instead of just blurting it out. Asking for permission is a sign of respect that can quickly shift the mood from an argument to a discussion.

3. Show compassion and ask for forgiveness. If the conversation is about something that white people in general have done, it can be helpful to say, "What we have done is so wrong. Can you please forgive us?" If it's something an individual white person said or did, you can say, "What happened to you was awful. I am so sorry they did that to you, and I pray that you can forgive them for being so mean." This is so much more effective than saying, "That's just in your head. They probably would have treated me the same way." In either instance, you can be a part of reconciliation instead of reinforcing the same old ruts of racial differences between us.

Most white people I know are tired of hearing about race. They know that slavery and Jim Crow were awful, but they desperately want to get past that. They have worked hard to obtain whatever success they have, and they have their own scars from being treated unfairly by others. Most of all, they don't want to be considered racist. I probably know a couple of thousand white people by name, and I can't think of one of them who actively wants to keep African Americans down or who I think of as a racist. But I have been in plenty of situations with my friends who are African American and something that a white person says or does strikes me as incredibly offensive and downright racist.

I realize this is not an issue that will just go away. Regardless of what country or what time we are in, people in a minority will be slighted by people in the majority more often than not. Even when an offense is not motivated by the color of their skin (for example, when the other person is just plain rude to everybody or is having a very bad day), it can still seem that way, and the more it happens the more it seems like it is motivated by race. The older we get, the more obvious this can become. Regardless of whether you believe it or not, people of color have a long and a fresh record of insulting things done to them by white people, and it's offensive to suggest that their experience is not their experience.

Underlying this in America is the slavery issue. Slavery remains an issue because it was a part of our value system when our country was founded. Our nation's leaders had a choice to be unified by the promise of more land (and include the Southern states as one country) or by the promise of life, liberty, and the pursuit of happiness for all people (and only accept free states into the union). They chose land. They agreed that African Americans in the South only counted as three-fifths of a person and wrote this into our nation's charter. That cold-hearted calculation hurts, and it haunts us to this day. The fact that this happened so long ago does not take away the pain when you are coming to grips with it as an African American student in a history class. Especially when the vestiges of it can be felt in a criminal justice system that touches one out of three African American men or is experienced as a minority at college in the everyday rudeness of professors, other students, and store employees.

INAPPROPRIATE RELATIONSHIPS

You don't have to read the daily paper for long before you come across an article about a middle school teacher having a sexual relationship with one of the boys in her class, or a high school coach who had sex with one of the girls on his team. Some organizations and churches working in schools have established huge boundaries to avoid this risk. They restrict adults from having the cell phone numbers of students or from giving them rides or meeting them away from school. This makes sense in the elementary school or middle school context, but it robs students of relationships when they are needed most at the high school level.

To avoid temptation and any appearance of impropriety, a Jonathan Commitment should be restricted, as a general rule, to people of the same gender. Exceptions may arise, as with George Lenyo and Porscha Taylor, but I would encourage you to only allow these in exceptional circumstances. The sad reality is that most boys in poverty have more women in their lives than men and that most girls in poverty have grown men pursuing them incessantly. Our young men need more good men in their lives, and our young women don't need any more grown men whose motives may be questioned. Establishing a same-gender rule for Jonathan Commitments can help on both fronts.

WHERE RECOGNITION BELONGS

In his book *Good to Great: Why Some Companies Make the Leap . . . and Others Don't,* Jim Collins talks about a flywheel and the incredible amount of energy required to start it moving as a metaphor for what it takes for a company to go from good to great. To get a humongous flywheel moving, he writes,

> You push with all your might, and finally you get the flywheel to inch forward. After two or three days of sustained effort, you get the flywheel to complete one entire turn. You keep pushing, and the flywheel begins to move a bit faster. It takes a lot of work, but at last the flywheel makes a second rotation. You keep pushing steadily. It makes three turns, four turns, five, six. With each turn, it moves faster, and

then—at some point, you can't say exactly when—you break through. The momentum of the heavy wheel kicks in your favor. It spins faster and faster, with its own weight propelling it. You aren't pushing any harder, but the flywheel is accelerating, its momentum building, its speed increasing.[5]

Don't ever forget, and don't let the people in your church forget, that the principal and the teachers have been pushing at the flywheel for years to get it moving. You will play a pivotal role in giving that flywheel momentum, and you can fall into the trap of thinking that you pushed it all by yourself. Honor the people who have been doing this long before you showed up. Lift up those who show up at 7 a.m. and work past 7 p.m. every day of the week.

The school you love well will begin to show signs of success, and the media will want to report on what is happening. Use those times to tell stories about the teachers and community partners whose work you are supporting. Don't shy away from telling the inspirational stories of your church members and their impact, but always make it clear that they are supporting the great people that came before you and are there every day. Those schools, beaten up all the time in the media, and their community partners, fighting for grants and credibility, can use every boost they get in the media. Use those opportunities to tell their story first and foremost.

MONEY ISSUES

Schools have such persistent needs for small resources not in the budget—like field trips, new uniforms, science equipment, or bus transportation for sporting events—that the people may be tempted to see your church as the one-stop solution for all their financial needs. It's important to reiterate that you are here for relationships, not resources. As a caring partner though, you will want to help out with resources when you can.

Depending on the size of the school and your church, you should enter this partnership with some funds set aside to strategically support the school. Not less than $5,000 and not more than $15,000 for a school year should work as a starting point, although you can certainly do more than that as your partnership grows. By holding a consistent presence in the school and its leadership team meetings, the school liaison will hear of many opportunities to give in ways that the church will want to support. However, the liaison also will be asked to give for things that the church won't want to support.

Liaisons should be prepared to say, like a mantra, "We can only support those things that will help to build relationships between your students and our members." This is an excellent filter to apply with discipline so church resources are stewarded consistently for the purpose of the relationship. Otherwise, the church liaison may come to be seen by people in the school as arbitrary or unfair for funding some requests and not others when so many come their way. When requests that do build relationships are made, the liaison should say, "I don't know, but I will ask around and see if we can help." The funds and the decision should not be seen as the liaison's. This person should have someone on the church team to talk this over with; otherwise, funds may be given too freely or withheld too callously. Sometimes the liaison should personally take the need to individuals in the church instead of simply going to the church fund that has already been established. People may respond better to requests like buying winter coats for kids than to simply writing a check to support the ministry in general. Resources from the church can be quite helpful to the school, but these resources should be a distant second to the power of the relationships that come through the church.

Your church should treat the partnership like a special ministry of the church, providing opportunities for people to give to the partnership. People often give generously when this is done, including one member of Oak Pointe Church who gave $25,000 to help thirteen students who most epitomized the values of Cody get through their first year of college.

The money issue may also come up between you and a young David you want to be a Jonathan friend to, although this issue seems to concern the Jonathan's more than the David's. In making my commitment to Keyvon, my primary concern was that he would see me as his personal bank account. I didn't want to feel used, and I told him so the first day we went out to lunch. In the course of our entire relationship, I never did. To the contrary, I often wished I had more money to share with him than I was able to at the time.

In some ways, I ended up treating Keyvon very much like my own teenage children. I made sure to get him a nice present or two for his birthday and Christmas. When we got together for lunch, I gave him twenty to forty dollars if I had it in the budget. If his phone was disconnected, I went to the local phone store to pay his bill. There were times I took him grocery shopping, and I would tell him how much I had budgeted for the trip. If I said $100, he would pick up about $60 worth of groceries and tell me he was good. I would have to personally put other items in the cart to buy the whole $100 worth.

In other ways, I have not treated Keyvon like my own son. I pay my children's Christian school education, cell phone bills, car insurance and gas. I pay to keep a roof over their heads and make sure they are warm, well-fed and well-clothed. Keyvon rarely had any of these things, and the $20 cash and meals I shared with him often seemed paltry. In that light, it would be more accurate to say that I treated him more like my nephew than my son. If you are not prepared to treat a young person at least as well as your own niece or nephew, the commitment may not be a good thing for you to do.

What I tried to do with Keyvon was to help him keep some goals in front of him, and not to let things be huge financial obstacles to him when I could, like buying him a bus card when he didn't have a car. Sometimes, a small sacrifice from you can lead to a huge change for the David in your life. Financial needs in the $300 to $600 range can elude young people for years: a decent bed frame and mattress, driver's training, the first month's rent on an apartment, a good laptop computer. Your consistency— having your friend's back at critical times, even when it may cost you some money—will have a much bigger impact on their life than what it costs you. When your church does this as a body, the impact multiplies itself across hundreds of relationships spread throughout the school and the community and continues to have an effect for years and even decades later, as my dad's life as a teacher did for me. That's the Jonathan Effect.

MAKING THE HURT OF THE CITY PERSONAL

At Oak Pointe Church, those who have been involved at Cody have been transformed spiritually. "If you step outside your comfort zone and see the world in a way you have never seen before, it forces you to see the world differently," Kurt Alber says.

It forces you to see your need for God differently. When the people you're working with are struggling with something you've never struggled with before, you don't have advice. You don't have a solution. You have to share how you've learned how you've worked through your struggles. You take them to your source when you do that, which brings you to that source in the same way. It grows your faith to be struck by that kind of thing. That's the most powerful impact this work has.[6]

Billy Thrall sees the same thing in his work with churches throughout Arizona.

When we do take that risk, and jump out there into the other, the unknown, the community, that's when we pray. That's when I pray. I don't pray when I'm safe, other than a "Thank you, God" prayer. When I'm out there, it's a "Help me, God; I don't know what to do" prayer. So we pray different. When you partner with a school and the people are different or whatever is different, and you have to figure out how to be the love of Christ, that's, I think, where we grow. There's where we grow.

But even for people in the church who have not gotten involved in the school personally, the impact of the partnership can still be felt. According to Kurt,

Nobody at Oak Pointe watches the news the same way they did. If there's a shooting, the first question is whether it was on the west side. That shooting becomes different than any other shooting in the city to our whole church because that's where Cody is. And the reality of what happens, now it's not just "Oh, there's been another shooting in Detroit. I hear that every day." Now it's a personal thing. "Is there somebody there I know who could have been harmed?

Was it a Cody student?" That's the question I get over and over. Because they care. Churchwide, it changes that perspective. It makes the hurt of the city personal, and not just more information in the news.

Violence, senseless, stupid, horrible violence, may strike the school or neighborhood you choose to partner with. Your people and their relationships may cause problems, not just from differences of race or income but also from similarities in pride and personal shortcomings that we all struggle with. But your church's commitment will influence more than the person and school you serve. You and your church will be influenced at least as much. That too is the Jonathan Effect.

Caught

Winter went by before I heard from Keyvon again. I called and texted, but no response. When we got back together in the spring, he explained that he did not want to put me in danger when he was doing wrong. He had made it through the winter in his own apartment, far from the streets where he made his living. He also had a new girlfriend named Destiny and was spending more time at her house. On a warm spring evening when they were relaxing together, a sharp rap on the door shattered their peace.

"Detroit Police! Open up!" Police raided the home and found 31 grams of heroin. Keyvon spent the night in jail and then was released on his own recognizance. They didn't tell him the next steps, what to do or where to go. They just opened up his cell and sent him home. He didn't know what he'd been charged with or what he should do. He called me for the first time in months.

We went out for lunch at Popeye's the next day, and Keyvon didn't touch his food. As I ate mine, he said he felt like a door was closing on his life. I told him that it was, because he kept trying to do things his own way instead of aligning his life with God's plans for him. I challenged him to surrender his life to God. I had talked to him about God a lot in the past, but never asked him if he was ready to give his life to the Lord. At this point, I was sick and tired of seeing him hurt himself doing things his way.

Keyvon agreed that he was ready, and we prayed the sinner's prayer together right there in Popeye's. As we walked to my car, I told him that the Lord was going to bless him in abundance over the next few weeks because I had seen that happen with new believers, just like the father who kills the fatted calf when his prodigal son comes home (Lk 15:11-32). Even so, I was surprised by how fast and how abundantly God moved.

We went to a local community college to get Keyvon enrolled in something, anything that would look good to a judge. When the counselor said that the fastest and best way to get hired was to become a certified nursing assistant (CNA), I remembered that my wife's friends ran a school providing CNA training. The cost was $575, but the owners, Julie Anumba and Karen Baker, waived it for us and enrolled Keyvon in a course starting at 4 p.m. that afternoon. We drove to the gas station to fill up Keyvon's tank. As I pumped the gas, Destiny called. She had heard about unclaimed property from the state of Michigan and researched Keyvon's name. It turned out that he had a tax refund of $675 from two years ago waiting for him to claim. We went to Health Care Solutions, bought Keyvon some scrubs and signed him up. At 4 that afternoon, within three hours of giving his life to the Lord, Keyvon was sitting in class to become a CNA, the cost of which was given as a gift to him by complete strangers, and he still had a check for $675 on the way. I had seen a lot of people experience inexplicable blessings after giving their heart to the Lord, but the magnanimity of this experience still surprised me.

8

Pushing Through

When I started at the United Way in Detroit, I was responsible for creating strategies to help our city become more educationally prepared. The assembly line had been pioneered in Detroit almost one hundred years earlier, but it had long since failed to provide jobs to kids from Detroit the way it had for their grandfathers. Detroit's United Way had been one of the holdouts from the old system of United Ways dedicated to raising money and giving it to nonprofits without setting goals or an agenda for change. But our new CEO, Michael Brennan, was one of the founding architects of the national movement to create agenda-driven United Ways while he was working for the national office in Washington, DC. He was brought home to Detroit after the untimely death of Virgil Carr, the presiding CEO, to bring the new focus on results to the Motor City.

I liked to get to work by 7 a.m. so I could read Brennan's copies of the national newspapers and pray in the board conference room before others started showing up. The board room's huge mahogany table had become my holy place, and I walked around it most mornings from 7:30 to 8:00, asking God for help in how to create or choose strategies that would have the biggest impact on our city.

In the summer of 2008, just before the economic crash that roiled the nation, there was an article in the *Wall Street Journal* about General Motors' recent public commitment to launch a battery-powered electric vehicle by 2011 called the Chevrolet Volt. The front page article stated that the technology for delivering on that promise had not yet been developed, and that GM risked its future on this commitment. The journalist was clearly skeptical of GM's ability to deliver on the Volt, and of GM's future in general.[1]

Something about that article evoked indignation within me. I felt like it was up to me to pray that promise through. And so every day my prayers walking around that conference table were filled with prayers for the leaders and engineers of GM, declarations of God's word that "our latter days will be greater than our former" (see Hag 2:9) and that GM "can do all things through Christ Jesus" (see Phil 4:13). I prayed and prayed and declared and believed that GM would launch the Volt before 2011, that Detroit would become known as a city of innovation and breakthrough technologies and that thousands of people would come back to Detroit to work in these growing industries. No matter what else was going on in my life, at home or at work, my prayers around that conference table always included GM, Detroit, and this breakthrough.

About a year after doing that, we moved from an old office building into a newly renovated space with a wide-open floor plan, and all of our walls had floor-to-ceiling windows. There was no private place to pray. My prayer time at the office faded away, but God's answer didn't.

The following summer, Mike Brennan met with Mark Reuss, GM's new president of North America. He liked what he heard from Brennan about our work turning around the most challenging high schools, and a few weeks later he went on a tour of Cody's campus with Brennan and me. Mark talked with a couple of the principals, sat in on a class and then visited with some of the students. He heard their stories and the impact that Cody's transformation had had on them.

As I walked Mark to his car, he stopped in the vestibule and admired the brickwork in this seventy-year-old building and said, "There's a lot of life left in this school." I gave him a bear hug because his belief connected so deeply with mine. Then all alone in the doorway he said to me,

> GM owes this nation a huge debt because of how it helped us get through when we were down. And we are not going to repay that just by making better cars. We are going to do it by making Detroit a great city again, and we will never get there if we don't start giving kids a great education again. I know what it feels like to have to get smaller in order to get better. That's what you are doing with the schools here.[2]

Two months later Mike Brennan got a call asking us to meet Mark in his office to make his commitment official. GM was going to donate $27.1 million over five years to double the number of schools in our network and to double down on early childhood efforts in those same communities. This would be the largest grant in the history of the GM Foundation and the largest single grant on record in the history of the United Way in America.

On November 16, 2010, Mike Brennan and I met with Mark and Robert Bobb, the man in charge of Detroit Public Schools, in Mark's office atop the Renaissance Center in Detroit. Mark was late because he had been at the Hamtramck Assembly Plant that morning for the celebration of the first GM Volt to come across the assembly line, a car auctioned off to benefit the kids in Detroit's schools. As he talked about all that GM had done and had been through to get the Volt done, and all of the technology and innovation that was needed, it all came back to me how much I prayed for exactly what he was so thankful for. It was almost like he was reciting my prayers back to me. God had heard my cry and answered it in a bigger way than I could have imagined, and sealed that gift with his fingerprints all over the wrapping.

Call it coincidence, but I have trouble believing it was a coincidence that I prayed for the successful launch of the Volt for at least a year, only to end up celebrating that launch with GM's president of North America as he was about to sign the check signaling the largest philanthropic investment in GM's history—the very vision God had put on my heart. The odds have to be a billion to one or more.

Not only that, Detroit has become cool again, and thousands more people are coming to live and work downtown in a way that seemed inconceivable in 2008—or when in 2009 *Time* featured us on the cover as a failed American city. Real estate development in downtown Detroit has virtually doubled year over year every year since 2011, according to Eric Larson, CEO of the Downtown Development Authority, finally getting the city to the point that "city leaders have dreamed of and worked toward since the 1967 riots."[3]

PRAY UNTIL SOMETHING HAPPENS

I think most people, even people of little or no faith, have at least one experience in life when they threw up a prayer of desperation to God and had it answered. One of the most important aspects of making the Jonathan Commitment to a school or a young person is becoming desperate in prayer for your David. What will happen when God's people begin to pray fervently for schools, teachers, and students they are in loving relationships with?

Along with my kids, as I put them to bed each night, I pray for Keyvon. I pray with him when we are together. When I called him to tell him that I was fired from a job, he prayed for me right there on the phone. For years I have prayed that Keyvon would give his heart to the Lord, get married, get a good job, get into a good church, and successfully navigate the challenges he faced. So far, he has made it through every challenge, given his heart to the Lord, and gotten a good job. He hasn't gotten married or found a good church home yet, but we are still praying.

What I've learned about prayer, however, is that sometimes it's not so much about how it changes things around me as how it changes me. When I pray—I mean really pray—for people and situations throughout the day, I'm a much humbler person and more sensitive to the lives of the people around me. I am not the master of my fate and captain of my soul. I've tried that, and it makes me more of a task master and a jerk. Prayer puts things in God's hands, and I like the Creator's power more than my own.

Making a Jonathan Commitment will change you and your church too. At Roosevelt the people stopped being so nice. "I did a study on nice," Kip Jacob, pastor of SouthLake Church, says, "and it turns out it means to ignore." His people are leading much more textured, purposeful lives. "More people are coming to SouthLake now because they want to engage the culture and make a difference."

The difference is felt in more than just the people. "After Roosevelt, everything changed," Kristine Sommer says. "SouthLake was no longer exclusively about what happened inside the four walls anymore. The church had thirty-five acres, and Kip was planning on building more buildings on the campus, and all of a sudden that wasn't the plan anymore." SouthLake changed its focus from the growth of its campus to serving Roosevelt. How they do that has changed, but their focus hasn't.

You and your church will begin to feel the pain of the city in a way you have never felt before, and you will be more dependent on God than before. The school you serve and young people you befriend will continue to experience trials and trauma, but they will have you, your church, and your friends and others in their corner to help them overcome. They need you to pray until something happens, and to help them keep pushing through.

RENEWING THE RUINED CITIES

You will not change the community or city where your school is located. That work will be done by the David you befriend. I say this because that's what Jesus said. The first time he preached publicly, Jesus went into the temple, opened the scrolls and read from Isaiah 61:

> The Spirit of the Sovereign LORD is on me,
> because the LORD has anointed me
> to proclaim good news to the poor.
> He has sent me to bind up the brokenhearted,
> to proclaim freedom for the captives
> and release from darkness for the prisoners,
> to proclaim the year of the LORD's favor
> and the day of vengeance of our God.

How much freedom lies in those words for all who feel bound by low expectations, hurtful words, or a lack of opportunities around them! What will the Lord do for them? He will come

to comfort all who mourn,
    and provide for those who grieve in Zion—
to bestow on them a crown of beauty
    instead of ashes,
the oil of joy
    instead of mourning,
and a garment of praise
    instead of a spirit of despair.

But look how much more power lies in the promise that comes next.

They [those who grieve in Zion] will be called oaks of
    righteousness,
    a planting of the LORD
    for the display of his splendor.

They will rebuild the ancient ruins
    and restore the places long devastated;
they will renew the ruined cities
    that have been devastated for generations.

Our calling as followers of Christ is to live and be like him. We are called to provide for those who grieve in Zion. Just as Zion represented Jerusalem at the time Jesus read this, isn't it likely that Zion represents our cities today. We are to provide for those who grieve in Chicago and Baltimore, Ferguson, and Los Angeles. And those who grieve in those cities are often its most vulnerable children.

What will happen to those who are comforted? It's worth repeating. They will receive "a crown of beauty instead of ashes, the oil of joy instead of mourning, and a garment of praise instead of a spirit of despair." This won't happen just for their sake, but so they can turn their city around. They are the ones who

will rebuild the ancient ruins
　and restore the places long devastated;
they will renew the ruined cities
　that have been devastated for generations.

In the first Scripture Jesus preached from, he made it clear that it is our responsibility to comfort those in bondage and pain, and to show them a path to freedom. They in turn, not us, will rebuild their schools (the devastated places) and their cities.

Pastor Andy Stanley describes well what will happen when we do this. He calls it an invitation to significance.

This is an invitation to step outside of yourself. This is an invitation to be unique. This is an invitation to move in a direction most people are afraid to move in. This is an invitation to make sure that at the end of your life there is somebody to say, "Thank you. Because if it wasn't for you, this would not have happened. If it wasn't for your sacrifice, if it wasn't for your self-denial, if it wasn't for your money, if it wasn't for your time, if it wasn't for the fact that you took some of your passion and you directed it in the direction of my need, my life wouldn't be where it is today." In so many words, this was Jesus's invitation to his audience and ours: to live a life of purpose.[4]

When Jonathan made this commitment to David, he didn't merely change David's life, he changed the future of Israel. When we purposely and consistently become a friend like Jonathan to young people, we are not only helping them. We are helping their friends, their family, and the family they will lead one day.

There are thousands of young people like Brittany, Jerome, Keyvon, and Porscha in every city, and more than enough churches, companies, and people in them to ensure that they all have a Jonathan in their lives—giving them the hope, the connections, and the perspectives they need to win their battle against poverty. When you do this, you will change more than their lives—you will help them forge a better future for the next generation of young people in cities across America.

That's the Jonathan Effect.

Still Standing

A few weeks after completing his training to become a certified nursing assistant, Keyvon landed a job working the afternoon shift at St. Joseph's Home for the Aged, a nursing home a few miles east of his mother's house, where he was living with his girlfriend, Destiny, and his mother's boyfriend.

I called him the day after his first day on the job to find out how it went. This wasn't just any job. This was one he found on his own and had successfully completed training for. This was bigger than his high school diploma to me. I was so proud of him and eager to hear all of the details of the first day when I called.

Keyvon sounded almost comatose when he answered the phone. It was 1 p.m., two hours before his second day on the job began, and his listless "hello" screamed anguish to me. "Where are you?" I blurted.

"In the ER," he replied. He explained that he had gotten into an argument with his mother that morning, and her boyfriend coldcocked him in the nose, breaking it badly. He was going to have to miss the next couple days of work. Two steps forward, three steps back. Keyvon's kudos for his first day of work was a broken nose, a day in the hospital, and another bout with homelessness.

Maritza and I had $600 socked away for his first month's rent, so I met Keyvon the next day at an apartment building to help make sure he wasn't getting ripped off in his search for a new home. He and Destiny had spent the night at her aunt's house. He had an inch-long gash on the left side of his nose and a blood-red eye next to it. It hurt just to look at him.

Over the next few days none of the apartments they looked at worked out, but they eventually found a small home for rent that they liked. It was near a park and in the center of the city, not too far from where Keyvon's son lived with his mother. Keyvon gave the landlord $300 to hold the house for them and asked for a copy of the lease so that "my lawyer can take a look at it." He loved to call me his lawyer, which always made me smile and the student loan bills I was still paying off seem a little more worth it, if only for my one true and longest-lasting client.

The landlord did not have an extra copy of the lease, so she agreed to meet Keyvon and me in the parking lot of my job to go over the terms and get the signatures. She showed up in a Cadillac Escalade with oversized tires, expensive rims, and a very large man in the passenger seat. She got out and told Keyvon that she had decided not to lease it to him and was refunding his $300. Keyvon was nonplussed; he was used to people doing him wrong. I was indignant and accused her of a breach of ethics for canceling his lease because he exercised his right to have a lawyer look at a legal contract. Before I knew it, her very large friend was threatening to square off with me, and then Keyvon jumped in. Destiny bolted out of the car and got between us, yelling at us to let it go, punctuating it with a dig to let us walk away with a little dignity. "We don't want the ugly old house anyway," she said. Keyvon and I backed down and avoided a street fight over a lease agreement.

Keyvon and Destiny gave up looking for their own place. They went back to live with his mother, never discussing the fight that occurred with her boyfriend, who still lives with them. Destiny and Keyvon's mother have become good friends, creating a safe and good bond in the home. Together, they help Keyvon raise Keyvon Jr., who is living there most of the time now.

Keyvon has been pursuing a job at the Detroit Medical Center, Detroit's largest hospital system, showing up every few days just to remind them that he is still ready for work. They called him last week to tell him that they are ready to hire him, but they did a background check on him and can't. He has a warrant out for his arrest for the time he was picked up with drugs.

Keyvon is going to turn himself in, and I will represent him. He faces four years in prison, unless the judge grants him leniency under a program known as HYTA, which gives first-time offenders between the ages of seventeen and twenty-one a delayed sentence if they stay clean during the time of their probation.

At the time of this writing, I don't know what will happen next. I only know that Keyvon has always been a great dad to his son. I do believe he will achieve his destiny. He will be happily married with a good job and a son who graduates from college. I intend to be standing next to Keyvon when he does.

Epilogue

As this book goes to print, people across the nation are looking for answers in the Flint water crisis. How did so many people who could have stopped this catastrophe fail to prevent it from happening in the first place? Matthew Seeger, a professor of communications at Wayne State University in Detroit, has studied more than a hundred disasters, and he found that "Every one of those has warning signs and signals. There's no crisis that happens that's a completely surprising event—there are always warning signs and signals that something isn't right." But the problem is in our interpretation of the signals, a problem that's exacerbated when the people sending the signals don't fall into our social circle. Seeger goes on to say, "Sometimes the signals come from people we don't understand: outsiders, people with a different orientation, who speak a different language, who don't have access to the same channels. This is not a new phenomenon."[1]

Even without the water crisis in Flint or the hurricane in New Orleans, America's cities are suffering through an enduring catastrophe—a horrible storm of generational poverty, mass incarceration, heart-numbing crime, broken families, and haunting unemployment. McKinsey & Company has found that the lagging achievement levels of low-income students in America has resulted in a permanent recession in our nation's economy.[2]

When we as a nation turn our backs on the children growing up in this raging storm, are we any different than the Israelites cowering in fear of Goliath—a present-day giant standing on the hill saying, "This day I defy the belief on which America was founded"? Are we any different than the signers of the Constitution who failed to acknowledge that self-evident truths applied to all people, not just those who looked like them? As in Flint, do we fail to respond to this crisis because the people in it are "outsiders"—outside of our circle of friends, who share similar income and education levels, religious affiliation, or color?

I believe there are churches and people all over this nation whose stomachs turn at the injustice that has come to be taken for granted in America's cities. They are called to do something meaningful, but don't have the pathway, or perhaps the permission, to act. I have tried to make clear that no church is going to save a school, and no person is going to save a kid. But they can become good and loyal friends, and the friendship of a church with a school, as well as the friendships of its members with the students, can help the students achieve their destiny. A destiny in which their life is more textured and their perspective more seasoned with equal parts of justice and mercy.

This is what I have found in my friendship with Keyvon. He changed my perspective. I believed that schools were failing kids for lack of great principals and great teachers. But he would not have made it to graduation—regardless of how good his school was—without someone at home to keep pushing him back to school when his world was pulling him away from it. He would not be gainfully employed today without someone who remained in his life after graduation to make connections with employers for him, to give him advice and encouragement when he failed, and to help him find and secure training more feasible than the local community college. He needed someone to help him process his trauma, to extricate him from the entanglements of the criminal justice system, to pray with him, to tell him over and over "I'm proud of you," and to love him through it all. Without that friendship, Keyvon would be one of the 5.5 million "disconnected" young people between the ages of sixteen and twenty-four in our cities who are neither working nor going to school.

Without that friendship, I would be much different too. I would likely be in a much different place at work, still one of the education reformers fighting earnestly for more rigorous schools and not fully understanding why kids continue to drop out.

I would also be a much different person at home. My own children, all teenagers now, have spent almost half their lives praying for Keyvon. They have seen me spend time and money with him when I was short on both, and they think that I have become a much gentler person in the process. They see me as more aware of their feelings now, of being a better listener, of not making them feel like items on my to-do list. My wife and kids are clear that my friendship with Keyvon has helped me to be a better husband and dad. I have come to see that as much as I have tried to help Keyvon fulfill his destiny, he has been instrumental in helping me achieve mine.

WHAT'S NEXT?

This is the opportunity that lies ahead for you. There are 172.8 million Christians in America.[3] Only one in thirty needs to make a Jonathan Commitment of their own to become a friend to every one of the 5.5 million disconnected young people in America. If you are one of those who hear that calling, you may want to check out one of the following organizations, each of which has a national reach and contact information for people who want to help.

- BeUndivided (beundivided.com) envisions 300,000 churches serving 100,000 schools by asking the question "How can we help?" and is committed to inspiring and equipping them to do so.

- Christian Community Development Association (ccda.org) has a mission to inspire, train, and connect Christians who seek to bear witness to the kingdom of God by reclaiming and restoring underresourced communities.

- City Serve (cityserveaz.com) works nationally to transform cities by fostering collaboration and relationships of care.

- National Church Adopt a School Initiative (churchadopta school.org) equips church leaders and volunteers with the necessary tools to conduct community outreach programs scalable to each church or organizational size.

- Young Life (younglife.org) is active in every city and works through school and community-based partnerships to introduce adolescents to Jesus Christ and to help them grow in their faith.

If you need some additional inspiration, you may want check out *UnDivided* on Netflix or *Life in Osborn* on YouTube.

Acknowledgments

To my mom, Julie Tenbusch, who chose to stay in our neighborhood in Detroit when most of the folks who looked like her moved out. You have always been Christ's love in action, and there would be no story here without you.

The best friends a guy could have, all of whom reviewed early drafts of this book and propelled me forward when things got tough: Tonya Allen, Gerry Boylan, Fr. Frank Canfield, SJ, Kevin Hofmann, Johnathon Matthews, Tonya Roberson and Dan Varner. I count on each of you for love and laughter in every conversation. A special thanks to my good friend, David Hecker, for trenchant insights at the end.

The amazing people who make good things happen for kids every day at Cody, especially principals LaToya Hall-King and Michelle Parker, uniquely gifted leaders, along with Johnathon Matthews, who selflessly give of themselves every day. Much gratitude also to William Gray, John Hoskins and Belvin Lyles for the conversations and perspectives that kept challenging me to write.

The entire team at IVP and especially my editor, Helen Lee. You are a prayer answered. You saw what I could not see and gave me the perfect blend of guidance, freedom and challenge to get there.

The love of my life, my wife, Maritza. If God had shown me who my wife was going to be when I was a child, I would have figured out a way to skip all of the years until the day I met you. This book was forged out of your prayers, your love for God and his people, and your love for me. Thank you for never giving up on me. *Te amo con todo mi ama y con todo mi corazón.*

And to our children, Grace, Julia and Jacob, who gave up so much—with joy and understanding—so that this book could be written. May God bless you in unique and wonderful ways, as you bless me all the time.

Ad majorem Dei gloriam.

Notes

PREFACE

[1]The concept of "escape velocity" was coined by Geoffrey Canada, founder of the Harlem Children's Zone, and discussed in Paul Tough's book about him, *Whatever It Takes*. Canada found that running after-school programs and other activities worked for a while for young people, but eventually the streets and poverty pulled them back down. He created a continuum of services in Harlem, from prenatal care to charter schools to help all kids from Harlem succeed in life. The principles in this book are intended to create similar results in less costly and relational ways.

CHAPTER 1: ALONE IN THE WILDERNESS

[1]Robert Balfanz, "More Information on The Methodology, Data, and Terms Used in the AP Dropout Factory Story," accessed May 2, 2016, *Center for Social Organization of Schools*, http://web.jhu.edu/CSOS /images/AP.html.

[2]Michelle Alexander, *The New Jim Crow: Mass Incarceration in the Age of Colorblindness* (New York: New Press, 2010), 13.

[3]Ibid., 6-7.

[4]Tammy Coxen et al., "Detroit's Untapped Talent: Jobs and On-Ramps Needed, Corporation for a Skilled Workforce, *JPMorgan Chase*, January 2016, www.jpmorganchase.com/corporate/news/pr/document/csw-chase -report-untapped-talent.pdf.

[5]Emma Lazarus, "The New Colossus," 1883.

[6]John Owens, *Confessions of a Bad Teacher: The Shocking Truth from the Front Lines of American Public Education* (Naperville, IL: Sourcebooks, 2013), 204.

CHAPTER 2: THE JONATHAN COMMITMENT

[1]See more about the Netter Center for Community Partnerships, University of Pennsylvania, at their website: www.nettercenter.upenn.edu.

[2]Billy Thrall, conversation with the author, February 2, 2016. All subsequent quotations by Billy are from the same conversation.

[3]Charles Murray, *Coming Apart: The State of White America, 1960-2010* (New York: Crown Forum, 2012), 23-99.

[4]Elizabeth Kneebone, Carey Nadeau, and Alan Berube, "The Re-Emergence of Concentrated Poverty: Metropolitan Trends in the 2000s," *Bookings Institute*, November 3, 2011, www.brookings.edu/research/papers/2011 /11/03-poverty-kneebone-nadeau-berube.

[5]Reed Jordan, "Millions of Black Students Attend Public Schools That Are Highly Segregated by Race and by Income," *Urban Institute*, October 30, 2014, www.urban.org/urban-wire/millions-black-students-attend-public -schools-are-highly-segregated-race-and-income.

[6]Murray, *Coming Apart*, 306 (emphasis added).

[7]Terri Peters, "'Blind Side' Mom Is Proud of Son's 'Amazing Journey' to Second Super Bowl," *Today*, February 4, 2016, www.today.com/parents /blind-side-mom-proud-son-s-second-super-bowl-appearance-t71416.

[8]This was taken from a student's Facebook newsfeed posted November 15, 2015.

[9]See, for example, Valentina Nikulina, Cathy Spatz-Widom, and Sally Czaja, "The Role of Childhood Neglect and Childhood Poverty in Predicting Mental Health, Academic Achievement and Crime in Adulthood," *American Journal of Community Psychology*, November 30, 2010, http://onlinelibrary.wiley.com/doi/10.1007/s10464-010-9385-y/full.

[10]Malcolm Gladwell, *The Tipping Point: How Little Things Can Make a Big Difference* (New York: Little, Brown, 2000), 12-13.

[11]"Disconnected Youth," *Social Science Research Council*, accessed May 3, 2016, www.measureofamerica.org/disconnected-youth.

[12]"Indicators of Higher Education Equity in the United States: 45 Year Trend Report," Pell Institute for the Study of Opportunity in Higher Education and the University of Pennsylvania's Alliance for Higher Education and Democracy, February 2015, 12, 31, www.pellinstitute.org /downloads/publications-Indicators_of_Higher_Education_Equity_in _the_US_45_Year_Trend_Report.pdf.

[13]Thomas A. Kochan, David Finegold, and Paul Osterman, "Who Can Fix the 'Middle Skills' Gap," *Harvard Business Review*, December 2012, https://hbr.org/2012/12/who-can-fix-the-middle-skills-gap.

[14]See the evaluation summary from Blueprints for Healthy Youth Development at www.blueprintsprograms.com/evaluation-abstract/big-brothers-big-sisters-of-america.

CHAPTER 3: THE CHURCH AWAKENING

[1]Robert Fogel, *The Fourth Great Awakening and the Future of Egalitarianism* (Chicago: University of Chicago Press, 2000).

[2]John S. Dickerson, *The Great Evangelical Recession: Six Factors That Will Crash the American Church . . . and How to Prepare* (Grand Rapids: Baker, 2013), 21-35.

[3]Ibid., 103.

[4]Ibid., 104.

[5]Steve Corbett and Brian Fikkert, *When Helping Hurts: How to Alleviate Poverty Without Hurting the Poor and Yourself* (Chicago: Moody Publishers, 2009), 45, citing George Marsden, *Fundamentalism and American Culture* (New York: Oxford University Press, 1980).

[6]Fogel, *Fourth Great Awakening*, 24.

[7]Ibid., 121-36.

[8]For a more in-depth history and summary of the principles of CCDA, see Wayne Gordon and John M. Perkins, *Making Neighborhoods Whole: A Handbook for Christian Community Development* (Downers Grove, IL: InterVarsity Press, 2013).

[9]Corbett and Fikkert, *When Helping Hurts*, 161.

[10]Bill Collins, interview with the author, June 26, 2015.

[11]Kevin Palau, *Unlikely: Setting Aside Our Differences to Live Out the Gospel* (New York: Howard Books, 2015), 1.

[12]Ibid., 1-95.

[13]Kip Jacob, telephone conversation with the author, April 16, 2015. All subsequent quotations by Kip are from the same conversation.

[14]Jerome Smith, telephone conversation with the author, February 5, 2016.

[15]Jeff Martin, telephone conversation with the author, February 3, 2016.

[16]Bob Shirock, coversation with the author, November 17, 2014.

[17]Charles Murray, *Coming Apart: The State of White America, 1960–2010* (New York: Crown Forum, 2012), 306.

CHAPTER 4: STARTING STEPS FOR BUILDING CHURCH-SCHOOL PARTNERSHIPS

[1]Chris, conversation with the author, September 16, 2014.

[2]Brock Shiffer, phone conversation with the author, February 3, 2016.

[3]Kristine Sommer, conversation with the author, January 26, 2016. All subsequent quotations by Kristine are from the same conversation.

[4]You can order this for your church and school through BeUndivided at beundivided.com/action-plans/sweatshirt-program.

[5]This "cultivation event" is taken from the Benevon model for fundraising. For more information, see the Benevon website at www.benevon.com.

CHAPTER 5: HOW YOU CAN CHANGE A LIFE

[1]Chip Heath and Dan Heath, *Switch: How to Change Things When Change Is Hard* (New York: Penguin Books, 2010), 227-28.

[2]Carol Dweck, *Mindset: The New Psychology of Success* (New York: Ballantine, 2008), 57.

[3]Ibid., 10.

[4]See Abigail and Stephen Thernstrom's seminal book for the charter school movement, *No Excuses: Closing the Racial Gap in Learning* (New York: Simon & Schuster, 2003), 94, citing Laurence Steinberg, *Beyond the Classroom: Why School Reform Has Failed and What Parents Need to Do* (New York: Simon & Schuster, 1996), 91, 161.

[5]"ASEP Issue Brief: Information on Poverty and Income Statistics," *U.S. Department of Health and Human Services*, September 12, 2012, http://aspe.hhs.gov/hsp/12/PovertyAndIncomeEst/ib.shtml.

[6]This statistic is taken from a study in Great Britain about the relationship between different types of family structures and physical abuse of children in them. If a child is living alone with a biological mother, the rate of abuse is fourteen times higher than with married, biological parents. If a child is living with cohabiting adults, the rate of abuse is thirty-three times higher. If the child is living alone with the father or alone with biological parents who are not married but cohabitating, the rate is twenty times higher, which is the number I cite in the text. See Patrick F. Fagan, "The Child Abuse Crisis: The Disintegration of Marriage, Family and the American Community," *Heritage Foundation*, May 15, 1997, www.heritage.org/research/reports/1997/05/bg1115-the-child-abuse-crisis.

[7]Johnathon Matthews, conversation with the author.

[8]William Julius Wilson, *More Than Just Race: Being Black and Poor in the Inner City* (New York: W. W. Norton, 2009), 90-92.

[9]Paul J. Zak, "The Trust Molecule," *Wall Street Journal*, April 27, 2012, www.wsj.com/articles/SB100014240527023048113045773657829953 20366.

[10]"David Kennedy of Police Legitimacy, Networks and Crime," *NYU Marion Institute of Urban Management*, March 6, 2014, http://urbanization project.org/events/detail/david-kennedy#.VbtWWflViko.

[11]Johnathon Matthews, conversation with the author.

[12]Paul Tough, *How Children Succeed: Grit, Curiosity, and the Hidden Power of Character* (New York: Houghton Mifflin Harcourt, 2012), 53-54.

CHAPTER 6: THE PLAN IN ACTION

[1]All of these figures are publicly available at the state of Michigan's website for school data, the Center for Educational Performance and Information, www.michigan.gov/cepi. It is worth noting that DPS's actual retention rate when combined with the six high schools that moved into the EAA was actually a much more abysmal 30 percent in 2013.

[2]Porscha Taylor, conversation with the author, June 3, 2016.

[3]John Browne and Robin Nuttall, "Beyond Corporate Social Responsibility: Integrated External Engagement," McKinsey&Company, March 2013, www.mckinsey.com/insights/strategy/beyond_corporate_social _responsibility_integrated_external_engagement.

[4]Mark Reuss, interview with the author at GM headquarters, June 2, 2015. All of the following comments by Mark in this chapter are from the same interview.

[5]Tim Higgins, "Reuss Walks GM Tightrope 20 Years After Father's Firing," *Bloomsberg*, October 24, 2012, www.bloomberg.com/news/articles/2012 -10-24/reuss-walks-gm-tightrope-20-years-after-father-s-firing.

[6]Mike DiGiovanni, conversation with the author, December 5, 2014.

[7]"Against All Odds: Cody High School's Journey to Success, This Is Brittany's Story," *WXYZ Detroit*, March 30, 2015, www.wxyz.com/news/region /detroit/against-all-odds-cody-high-schools-journey-to-success-this-is -brittanys-story.

[8]Dawin Wright, conversation with the author, July 23, 2015.

[9]Brittany Agee, conversation with the author, April 27, 2015.

CHAPTER 7: WHAT TO WATCH OUT FOR

[1]Johnathon Matthews, quoted in "Much Love: The Story of the Detroit School Turnaround," *United Way*, accessed June 9, 2013, https://vimeo .com/68299974.

[2]Steve Corbett and Brian Fikkert, *When Helping Hurts: How to Alleviate Poverty Without Hurting the Poor and Yourself* (Chicago: Moody Publishers, 2009), 64-65.

[3]Ibid., 65.

[4]Ibid., 115-19.

[5]Jim Collins, "Good to Great," *Fast Company*, October 2001, www.fast company.com/43811/good-great.

[6]Kurt Alber, conversation with the author, January 14, 2016. All subsequent quotes by Kurt are from the same conversation.

CHAPTER 8: PUSHING THROUGH

[1]Holman W. Jenkins Jr., "What Is GM Thinking?," *Wall Street Journal*, updated July 2, 2008, www.wsj.com/articles/SB121495482307421193.

[2]This meeting and conversation with Mark Reuss took place on September 26, 2010.

[3]Louis Aguilar, "It's Boom Time for Developments in the Heart of Detroit," *Detroit News*, January 8, 2016, www.detroitnews.com/story/business /real-estate/2016/01/08/development-boom-detroit/78447964.

[4]Andy Stanley, sermon titled "Re:Solution: Something to Show for It," North Point Community Church, January 10, 2015, http://northpoint.org /messages/resolution/something-to-show-for-it.

EPILOGUE

[1]Matthew Seeger, quoted in Nancy Kaffer, "When Empathy Dies: How Everyone Failed the People of Flint," *Detroit Free Press*, February 21, 2016, www.freep.com/story/opinion/columnists/nancy-kaffer/2016/02/20 /flint-government-crisis/80414296.

[2]"The Economic Impact of the Achievement Gap in America's Schools," *McKinsey on Society*, April 2009, http://mckinseyonsociety.com/the -economic-impact-of-the-achievement-gap-in-americas-schools.

[3]"America's Changing Religious Landscape," *Pew Research Center*, May 12, 2015, www.pewforum.org/2015/05/12/americas-changing-religious -landscape.

About the Author

Mike Tenbusch is the CEO of Uncommon Solutions, LLC, a consulting firm helping urban schools, churches and impact organizations create strategies to improve conditions and outcomes for kids. Born and raised in Detroit, he has had a lifelong calling to make Detroit a better place to be a kid and to raise a family. A graduate of the University of Michigan Law School, he cofounded an organization that now serves fourteen thousand children each year, served on the board for Detroit Public Schools, helped a charter school district graduate more than 90 percent of its first high school class, created a plan and led the effort to turn around the city's most challenged high schools, and launched a training center for young people in partnership with bestselling author Mitch Albom. He and his wife, Maritza, live with their three children outside Ann Arbor, Michigan.

Email him at mtenbusch@uncommonsolutionsllc.com.